COMMON SENSE

Booklocker.com, Inc.
2004

COMMON SENSE

by

Jon Clerry

Table of Contents

Jon Clerry

Preface

Everybody has heard the term common sense and everybody has heard that only a few people have it. But just what is common sense. Let me forward a definition that I feel will prove valid. Common sense is applying knowledge that has been learned elsewhere to a similar situation in a totally different field. For example if you know what works for automobile insurance you may be able to apply what you've learned there to a totally different field such as medical insurance. Seeing the parallels and knowing when to apply them is what I'll define as common sense.

What I am offering in this book is a wide variety of problems that are begging for a solution with the common sense answer to these problems. The beauty of a common sense solution is that most people, regardless of their education, can see the correctness of the solution once they see how the solution is working elsewhere on a similar problem. Common Sense solutions are offered on subjects as varied as the Iraq War, how to solve the problem of medical insurance for everyone, and how to prevent child abuse in childcare centers.

If you can keep an open mind and not let political bias come in to your thinking I think you will agree with the solutions offered. It is my prayer that God will use this book to heal some of the arguments this nation is bogged down with because of political prejudice. An eclectic array of problems is offered so the reader can see how the answers given by common sense are free from political bias by virtue of simply using things found to be true in other situations that apply to the situation in question.

The challenge is to keep political bias out of the picture. For example if you are a Democrat all contradictory arguments offered by Republicans are viewed as erroneous. All the Current proponents of John Kerry are anti-war regardless of what their original views might have been. And all the current proponents of John Kerry are pro-choice regardless of how they were brought up or what their moral teachings would dictate. And of course the reverse is true for Republicans backing George Bush. But there is only one correct answer to the questions of our day and age. Common sense can be used to tear away political bias and get at what it is.

Chapter 1
THE WAR IN IRAQ

We are in the middle of a fight against terrorists and to our dismay we find that the non-democratic nations of Islam see things differently than we do. Opinion Poles of Islamic people living in countries that are not democracies show they don't like us and they do not feel remorse over the terrorist attacks we have suffered. Looking over seas to Israel they have an identical situation where the Palestinians feel Israel is to blame entirely for their problems.

There are numerous parallel situations from history. Look at the Civil war in the US where one of the major contributors to the war was a difference in how the South and the North viewed slavery. Look at the civil rights movement and the differences between the KKK and the Black Man. From World War Two days look at the Nazis and the Jews. And also from World War Two look at the Japanese and their view of superiority over the white race. All are bigotry caused by one group singling out another as inferior or unworthy. All represent blindness on the part of the individuals or organizations of any given cause because they "know" their cause is right and just.

Islam in the backward countries that have not emerged into democracies is much like the Japanese in World War Two. The people of non-democratic Islam see all other religions and peoples as inferior and evil. We can not win by trying to prove we are right because in their eyes we can never be right. With Japan we finally won by showing them that continued fighting would end their existence. As long as Japan thought they had a possibility of winning we had no way to stop them. They saw their cause as right and just. And since Islam in the non democratic Islamic countries sees their cause as right and just we may not be able to change their behavior unless and until their very existence is about to end. Unfortunately though even knowing your enemy can annihilate you is not always enough. A prime example of continuing on even when you know your enemy can annihilate you is the behavior of the Palestinians in Israel.

If we allow things in the non-democratic Islamic world to continue on their current path, the day is fast approaching when the situation will threaten our very existence. All that has to happen is for these countries to develop nuclear capability. It is simply a matter of time until that happens. Matter of fact Pakistan which has developed nuclear capability has shared nuclear secrets with non-democratic

Islamic countries. Hence something needs to be done and it needs to be done quickly. The current war being waged on terrorism may be the answer but in my opinion it won't be enough. It appears that we are to non-democratic Islam what Israel is to the Palestinians. If so the problem will continue even after the terrorists are eliminated.

We could bomb the non-democratic Islamic world out of existence. Based on what happened to Japan they would probably benefit in the end because it would give them a chance to begin again. However I think we would all agree this is not a desirable way to resolve the problem. I do feel we could benefit however by getting the leadership of non-democratic Islamic countries to wake up to this possibility. This approach certainly worked for our Cold War with Soviet Russia. Russia was held at bay by the realization of mutual destruction. If we can get the leaders of the non-democratic Islamic countries to accept this as a real possibility the way Soviet Russia did they may rethink what they are teaching their people. However common sense based on what happened in the US Civil War and Japan in World War Two says they may still feel their way is right and press on with righteous fervor to have their definition of Good conquer their definition of Evil. The threat of annihilation may be insufficient until it's too late and they realize it is actually happening.

Another way to help our situation would be to have the whole world recognize that Islam's intolerance of the rest of the world as practiced in non-democratic Islam is out and out bigotry. We should refuse to accept this kind of behavior any more. Ostracizing the bigots of the civil rights conflict has forced them to change their views as they realized the rest of the world was not accepting them. For example we should not honor their attempts to keep us from practicing our customs and religious beliefs while we are in their country. And we should cease to be sensitive to their bigoted views while they are in the rest of the world. After all who is it that is laying down these ridiculous laws anyway. Their governments are small and don't represent the people and should not present a problem when we ignore their stupid laws.

We constantly live in fear of hurting their feelings. This elevates their feelings to a right and gives them credibility. We don't need to be callous, just matter of fact expecting them to behave as adults and respect the fact that others have rights too. Besides, forcing their people to see that there are at least two sides to the story may eliminate their closed society that is similar to Japan and Germany in World War Two. In a closed society you can eventually get everyone to believe whatever lie you may be telling. In an open society the conflict of differing opinions eventually brings about discussion and new realizations of what is right and wrong. Right now before the leaders of non-democratic Islam have nuclear capability is the time to ignore their bigotry and refuse to honor their insistence that we not practice our beliefs in their countries.

I have heard the argument that a big part of the problem is the difference in economic level between the non-democratic Islamic countries and the US. Common Sense however would indicate this is not the reason for our problem. If it were we would have the same problem from every Third World Country in existence. Admittedly raising their standard of living might help them feel better about themselves but as witnessed by Germany and Japan in the Second World War, feeling good about one's self doesn't eliminate bigotry.

Cutting off our dependence on the non-democratic Islamic World's oil supply would on the surface appear to cause a deepening of the problem. The increased isolation causing a more closed society and the additional reasons to hate us would certainly work against us. But maybe we are looking at this wrong. The leaders are the ones who would feel the oil freeze the most. What if we give the leaders a deadline of some date in the near future when we will stop using their oil unless they change the way they are guiding their people. If we put real teeth into this by laying out a plan to not use their oil and if we laid out a plan to monitor what is being taught and said in their schools, news media, and other government controlled information, we could bring about major changes.

The greatest potential for correcting the problem however is none of the above. Looking at Germany and Japan as the example, the problem finally went away when we set up a democracy in their midst. In Japan the example is of a whole country being forced into an American style democracy. The only way we could duplicate this is to forcibly take over all the non-democratic Islamic countries and put democracies in place. This is impractical to say the least and totally undesirable from the standpoint of what such a takeover would cost both sides. But based on what happened in West Germany, this is not required. The existence of an American style democracy in West Germany eventually solved the problem for all of Germany. Although the East Germans came from a Nazis environment where America was a hated enemy and continued on with a communistic state where America was still hated, they fell in love with our style of life and readily adopted it as their own. The East Germans were close enough to the working model to see that it was something they wanted. Matter of fact, looking at the spin off into the Soviet Republics there is hope that a similar spin off would affect many countries with animosity toward America.

One additional benefit of a democracy is the checks and balances provided by permitting opposing political views to be openly discussed. It operates similar to the silent hand mentioned by Adam Smith when discussing how the free market place prevents someone from getting too far out of line on pricing etc. Any time one faction gets too extreme the open discussion permitted in a democracy keeps it from getting too far out of line.

The approach being used by the Bush administration follows closely this thinking and I believe their approach is the best possible for solving the problem. The problem with the anti-war approach is you allow things to worsen until something totally unacceptable like the use of nuclear devices by terrorists happens. The consequences of one well placed nuclear device in a city such as New York or Washington is beyond imagination. One certain consequence would be the failure of our current economic system. And the millions of displaced people and the destruction of infrastructure would be beyond what our political system can handle. The impact on our existence would be totally devastating. Regardless of whether we think we could survive such an attack, everyone needs to recognize this scenario must never be allowed to play out. We must not fall for the anti-war approach where we would be waiting for such a scenario to happen before going to war.

So far as justification for declaring war on militant Islamic terrorists, the tragedy of 9/11 is at least as good a reason to declare war as the attack on Pearl Harbor by Japan. Declaring war on Ben Laden and his cronies does nothing toward eliminating the overall problem. It would simply be eliminating one of many armies put forth by the militant Islamic movement. The war had to be declared against all who support this movement. Although Iraq itself did not perform the 9/11 attack, they stand as a perfect example of the non-democratic Islamic systems that are breeding these militant Islamic terrorists. And Iraq represents the perfect place to insert a West German type situation to initiate healing in the same fashion as what happened with East Germany. In other words we had a solution that needed to start working before the unthinkable happens and Iraq represented the perfect place to initiate that solution. Whether or not Iraq had weapons of mass destruction is of far less importance than whether Iraq was the best place for insertion of an American style democracy and whether regime change could be justified.

To all who say we needed to wait for some kind of attack from Iraq against this country (such an attack would have never come; terrorists with no tie to any one country would continue to be the attackers) I say the price for such methodology is too high. I don't want to wait until we lose millions instead of thousands to the ridiculous struggle being waged against us by militant Islamic terrorists. We could literally justify an attack on all non-democratic Islamic countries that offer support to these terrorists but the regime change in Iraq makes a lot more sense. And regime change in Iraq is a far better option than doing nothing, which is suicidal.

What most anti war proponents fail to realize is that the problems with the non-democratic Islamic countries and Islamic terrorists will not go away on it's own. Left alone the way anti war proponents suggest, terrorism would become a huge cancer with terrorist acts escalating exponentially throughout the free world. And the wall separating militant Islam from America and Israel would become impenetrable. Eventually the differences would lead to annihilation of one or the other society. The effects on America would make current events look like a walk in the park. Literally millions in America would lose their lives and our financial and political systems would fail. In a book describing how to bring America to it's knees, Chinese military experts lay out the methodology being used by militant Islam terrorists.

In the long run the anti-war approach would lead to much more blood shed both in this country and in the countries supporting the terrorists. First we would suffer the unavoidable huge attack on us. Such an attack is avoidable only if we go on the offense and keep the terrorists occupied on their own soil.. You have to put them on the defensive before you can hope to foil their plans. Second the non-democratic countries of Islam would suffer much larger losses of life as we are forced to finally retaliate against an enemy that seems to be coming from all of them. The course that the Bush administration took was by far the course of least loss of life for both sides.

The way the Bush administration has maneuvered in and around so many dangerous options has been miraculous. Poor handling could have led to all out war with all the non-democratic Islamic countries. Instead by going after someone that everyone recognized as a criminal the other non-democratic Islamic countries have been able to avoid having to declare war. Weapons of Mass Destruction were not a requirement to launch an attack on Iraq. They were instead a good reason to argue for such an attack with peoples who have no vested interest in ending the militant Islamic terrorist onslaught against Israel and America. And by inserting a democracy in their midst, all non-democratic Islamic countries now realize their time is limited and they can't do anything about it. They are caught up in a proverbial catch 22. If they try to over turn what we've accomplished they will lose control over their people. And if they don't do something to over turn what we've accomplished they will lose control over their people. The die is cast. Militant Islam is about to come to an end as the people of non-democratic Islam discover we are not the great Satan but rather people they want to emulate. The question now is have we done all this in time to avoid the unthinkable happening to our country. Thank God we didn't wait any longer to act.

We are just now beginning to get a glimpse of the long-range benefits of the war on Iraq and terrorism. Look at how Libya threw open their nuclear weapons plans to avoid the US attacking Libya the way we did Iraq. And look at how Hamas backed away from their threat against the US when the US responded with targeting Hamas leaders. They literally fell back in fear realizing we could and would eliminate their leadership in the way we did in Iraq and Afghanistan. No longer do the Militant Islam organizations scoff at our capabilities. They now realize we mean what we say. And for once they are listening.

Chapter 2

CRITICIZING THE COMMANDER AND CHIEF

Negative of any kind will destroy. Just let the members of a church congregation start questioning the minister. Or let the employees at a given company start questioning their management. If you don't believe this, try doing service work for someone who is paying for your services. Then turn a critic loose on how good your work really is. Or bringing the argument closer to home, what if your boss gave an open ear to anyone that did not like you? Would the constant criticism of your work by your enemies raise questions that would be better left unanswered? I promise I can bring you down by asking negative questions daily about your work. Unless your boss is results oriented he or she will develop poorer opinions of you as they hear your activities repeatedly questioned and criticized.

We've all participated in sports contests. Either as spectators at our schools or as participants on an athletic team. If you get enough members on a team to question the wisdom of their coach you can defeat the team before they enter a game. Do you know any coach who doesn't have questionable practices etc. that could raise legitimate questions about his or her capabilities? Every coach has shortcomings. We've all learned from athletic contests that regardless of his or her shortcomings you don't criticize the coach during a game. Yet in America we are in a life and death struggle which is much more important than an athletic game. And although everyone realizes from athletics that you don't criticize the leadership during the game, we are openly criticizing our president and our leaders during the war on Iraq.

How do you get around the destructive power of negative? The only way involves those words that the Liberal Left tells you to avoid. Patriotism, faith, and confidence in your leadership cut through all this. According to the Liberal Left these are dangerous because you could follow your leader down the wrong path. And they are right if the basics the decisions are based on aren't sound. That's where those other unmentionables such as religious beliefs, morals, and character come in. Blind faith in Hitler led the Germans to destruction. But his religious beliefs, morals, and character were way off base to the point that he should never have been trusted in the first place. And there was no accountability with the German people the way there is in our system with checks and balances and elections every few years. The Liberal Left has locks on the situation both ways. First they don't want you to look at religious beliefs, morals and character in choosing your leaders. Then they tell you not to place trust in your leaders because that trust may be misplaced.   If we follow their guidelines they are correct that we can't place too much trust in our leaders. But if we go back to the founding principles of this country and select only men of faith with high morals and good character they are wrong. The only way you win at athletics, or life, or national endeavors is to trust your leaders so that you have confidence in where you are going and what you are doing. The time for questioning is when you review the results of the year or term; not every minute of the day.

How much good would it do a football team to openly question the ability of their coach as they enter the football field for a game. As anyone will tell you that would be disastrous. But isn't that what is happening in America when we openly question the abilities of the President while we are in a major war. It's ludicrous to think such actions are helping the country. The reason we have only one person in charge is that anything with more than one head is a monster. Two or more heads making a decision won't work. And constantly questioning the decisions a leader is making is destructive.

Too many critics questioning the decisions of our leaders destroy the effectiveness of our leadership. I've never seen a critic accomplish anything worthwhile. It is the people they are criticizing that are doing the great things. This country somehow needs to get off this ridiculous thing of allowing constant criticism of our elected leaders. I don't mind hearing from the people who are actually doing the work but constant input from the critics as to what he or she was "really" saying or what it "really" means is totally out of line. I have to laugh when the news spends hours interviewing retired this or that instead of simply asking the guy who is responsible. It would be great if we all limited our exposure to the news to just a few minutes a day and then only listened to the movers and the shakers instead of all the little guys running around trying to criticize them.

We've got to somehow put the critic back to the level he deserves. Whatever administration is in power when war happens was elected to that position. They need to be respected as the leaders of a great and unified country. Saying they are incompetent or belittling them constantly is demeaning to our country and destructive to our way of life. Treating our leaders as punching bags and openly humiliating them is getting way out of line. The people who are constantly telling us that everything is wrong when a war is going on need to be recognized as traitors. This is especially true for people in responsible positions. They are doing as much damage to this country as the terrorists. Legitimate criticism can be handled quietly in closed sessions of congress so that we present a unified front to our enemies. Open criticism of your coach during a football game would not be tolerated. Why then do we tolerate open criticism of our commander and chief during a war.

Chapter 3
MEDICAL INSURANCE

It's real clear why Uncle Sam can't solve the medical care dilemma. Too many people stand to make or lose too much money to let this simply slide by. Hence our congressmen are trying to please everyone and in the process not solving the problem. Have you ever wondered why the car insurance industry doesn't have the same problems? The reason is simple. The car dealers selling cars and the banks lending money on car sales use cars as collateral. If we used the same set up for car insurance that we have for medical insurance, the banks and car dealers would end up with worthless pieces of junk sitting by the side of the road whenever someone had a wreck that wasn't insured. Unfortunately nobody requires the human body as collateral for investments. Hence a body falling apart due to lack of medical insurance doesn't carry the same weight in congressional thinking.

First let's take a common sense look at what insurance is all about in the first place. The original intent of insurance was to prevent anyone from getting caught out on a long expensive limb. The idea is to spread the cost of medical care over a large number of people so that the excessive expenses of the unlucky few can be affordably covered by the many. What has happened is something entirely different. Over the years the insurance companies have tried to trim costs by spotting in advance the high-risk individuals who would spoil the curve. By eliminating these high-risk people they have cut costs and improved profits. The general public went along with this because it saved them all money. Besides the "other person" is always the one out on the limb rather than us. And the high-risk people can't afford to cry out against such practices. Of course we still pay the cost but not in insurance premiums. We pay when we get our medical bills, which are inflated to cover the losses to the medical community when patients can't pay their bill. We pay in taxes that cover the people who are destitute because they can't pay their medical bills, etc. We pay in lost productivity when people can't afford to get their medical problems solved. And most of all we run the very real risk of us or our loved ones paying by losing everything when we encounter a major illness not covered by insurance.

While at first glance not insuring people at high risk appears to make sense and save the general public money, closer investigation shows it defeats the whole purpose of insurance. First we assume that anyone worth his or her salt has insurance and therefore doesn't have to worry about this problem. "Only those who are welfare types" is the assumed group that is in trouble. However the facts show this is not the case.   You'll find yourself outside insurance protection if you fall in one of the following categories:

• You lose your job and can't carry your insurance with you

• Your insurance company goes out of business and you have a medical condition that prevents you signing on with another insurance company. Many insurance companies go out of business every year. I personally have had this happen to me twice in 10 years.

• You or someone in your family develops a mental illness (often these people become homeless because of lack of a way to pay for care).

• You work for a small business that doesn't provide medical insurance or you are self-employed and don't buy health insurance until it's too late.

It is far too easy to get caught outside the umbrella. The number of people in this country who don't have medical insurance is over 50million. In addition many cannot answer the medical questions honestly on an insurance application because no insurance company will touch them if they do. Frequently the information that makes them uninsurable is from private tests that no one else has the right to know. For example you may have paid a specialist a very large sum of money to perform special tests on you 5 or 10 years ago. These tests show some medical problem that no one could decipher otherwise. The problem is that any medical condition you develop prevents you from being insurable. Whatever causes you to lose your existing medical coverage then puts you outside the system.

Looking at what happens when these people become uninsurable shows we need to make major changes. First if you are caught on the outside it is obvious that a change is needed. But what if you remain covered and it's only "other people" who have the problem. When people cannot pay for health care we end up with huge losses or mistreatment of human beings or both at all hospitals. When the expenses become exorbitant as they usually do before we die, people lose all their possessions. This in turn affects the prosperity of our community. In extreme cases people become homeless, which hurts the whole community. And the resulting welfare expenses affect us all.

Why not use the example of the automobile accident repair industry to solve our medical care woes. As with cars we could require the insurance companies to insure everyone. This can be justified since most medical problems will fall on the state if the individual cannot afford to pay. If the insurance companies are permitted to deny insurance to someone because of their medical situation we eliminate the very benefit we are all after when we buy insurance. The insurance companies are protected from financial harm by being able to set their rates high enough to cover actual expenses as is now done with auto insurance.

We should not penalize the insured based on his health or past experience. Private medical records should be treated as private. You could possibly penalize for certain bad health habits such as smoking, hazardous hobbies or jobs, etc. but not the fact that you have been sick. To be fair, just like with car insurance, everyone should be required to buy insurance or accept being placed in a charity pool by the state if you cannot afford insurance.

Another thing that could be borrowed from the car insurance industry is the requirement to get competitive bids for treatment just like you do for car repairs. If you want to go with a higher priced outfit because you like their work better, you can if you pay the difference. This should go a long ways towards reducing medical expenses.

In summary the auto insurance industry has done a far better job of providing everyone with affordable insurance than the medical insurance industry. Why not use a little common sense and incorporate what's good about the car insurance business into medical insurance. This way we don't have to reinvent the wheel. We can simply copy a system that is working.

Perhaps we should look at the human body as collateral securing our country's prosperity like the car industry looks on the car as collateral securing that industry. If too many people fall outside the realm of health insurance and if too many people go bankrupt and lose all their possessions because of lack of health insurance, we will all lose our prosperity through this great country's financial system collapsing.

The common sense solution of copying a system that is working hasn't happened via congressional legislation. This is a classic example of too many interests at stake. I imagine the insurance industry would fight this solution because they would then have to justify their rates to too many government overseers but this is a much smaller problem than leaving huge numbers of people outside the protection of insurance. The medical community would probably not like the use of three competitive bids as in car repair. This would cause problems in keeping a patient unless you are willing to have competitive rates. But which is worse, escalating medical expenses which are bankrupting the nation or competition on rates.

In other words, it is easy to see why this problem has not been solved yet. There are simply too many competing interests. We need to take matters into our own hands and insist on this type of solution.

Chapter 4
LEGAL REFORMS

Imagine a civil case where the judge throws out the claims of the plaintiff as ridiculous, the damages sought as unjustifiable, and the lawyers bringing the suit are fined for unprofessional conduct by virtue of bringing such a case to court. Imagine a divorce proceeding where the judge questions both the husband and wife to determine if either had behaved as husband or wife. And based on the fact that both had failed in their marriage role decides that neither deserve any special consideration.

Shifting to the criminal side of the legal system, imagine you are accused of some traffic violation other than speeding and your side of the story is directly opposed to that of the police officer. Imagine further that the judge accepts your story with the same weight as the officers and the officer is required to prove his allegations.

On a more serious note imagine you are falsely accused of possession of drugs (maybe someone has hidden drugs in your car or home) and the judge demands that your property not be seized until your guilt or innocence can be determined. Imagine also that the court, the jury, and everyone in contact with the case assumes you are innocent until the prosecution can prove otherwise. Imagine still further that if you are found guilty the prison system recognizes the verdict may be in error and you are treated well while in prison. And if you are found innocent, imagine the state pays all your legal fees and the judge instructs everyone connected with you to reinstate employment or anything else lost while you were incarcerated.

If you were unlucky and happened to be tried by a strict fire and brimstone judge, imagine there was some legal authority you could go to to get your punishment reduced to a more fair judgment. At present none of the imaginings discussed above are realistic. All happen basically just the opposite of the way I've asked you to imagine them. The two legal systems, civil and criminal, each have their own problems. First let's address the civil system.

Pat Robertson once gave an excellent summary of what needs to change in our civil suits. The bible states an eye for an eye and a tooth for a tooth. At first glance the depth of wisdom in this statement is not obvious. But on further examination it says "only" a tooth for a tooth. Instead we see many exorbitant judgments that bear no relation to the value of the damages. People are being awarded millions of dollars for damages that are not worth anything like a million dollars. A prime example of the harm being done is what happened with the manufacture of private aircraft. The lawsuits were so ridiculous that the whole industry was destroyed. Lack of reasonable oversight and lack of accountability on the part of both lawyers and judges is responsible for this happening.

Additionally there is no penalty to the party bringing about the lawsuit if they are making an unjustifiable claim. Many suits are brought about knowing there is little or no chance of winning in court simply because the defendant involved will settle out of court to avoid the excessive expenses of hiring lawyers to defend against the claims. Lawyers should be held accountable for using good judgment in initiating suits. Every other profession is held accountable for using good judgment in their field of expertise. Holding lawyers to similar requirements would stop many unnecessary law suits. Their accountability should be similar to the cost that will be incurred by the defendant to defend against the charges. And Judges should be permitted to throw cases out which fall in this category. Naturally this judgment would be subject to appeal which would prevent one judge from causing undue harm to someone.

Moving on to the Criminal side of our legal system, one of the main problems is assumption of guilt rather than innocence. In minor offenses such as traffic violations the word of the officer of the law is always taken over that of the defendant. The officer should be required to prove his statements using video records, witness testimony, etc. Simply taking the officer's word over that of the defendant is an assumption of guilt rather than innocence.

Legal defense has become so expensive we need to revamp the way criminal justice is handled. All someone has to do to ruin you is plant a drug on your property and turn you in or accuse you of a crime. Literally you are no better off if you are innocent than if you are guilty. You will pay huge sums of money and you will probably lose your job just as starters. If a person is found innocent, he should not have to pay for his defense. After all, if he is innocent, the justice system is at fault for accusing him. Similarly individuals accused of crimes should have protection against losing their job etc. if they are found innocent. And since we are often wrong in our verdicts, there should be protection against undue hardship from having to pay exorbitant legal fees, etc. even when found guilty. Furthermore, since we are supposed to be assumed innocent until proven guilty, seizure of homes, cars, bank accounts, etc. should never be done just because we have evidence they were used in drug sales, etc. Acts of this nature should only come after a judge and jury have found the party guilty and the judge and jury have decided the extent to which property should be seized. As it is now families suffer undue hardships simply because a member of the family is accused of trafficking in drugs.

Further we need to realize that our track record of putting the right man behind bars is not good. Too often later evidence or DNA samples or some other happening prove we put the wrong man behind bars. This being the case, we need to make sure prisoners are treated humanely. Sexual abuse (especially where men gang rape male prisoners), rough treatment by inmates or guards, excessive punishment, etc. should be stopped. If we recognize that every man in prison may be there by mistake we will err on the safe side. I would rather treat a bad person too good than treat a good person too bad.

Although this will fly in the face of many, I believe we need to eliminate the death penalty for the same reason. At the very least the death penalty should be limited to cases where there are at least two trustworthy witnesses to the murder. The death penalty should never be permitted for circumstantial evidence. There is no "beyond a reasonable doubt" when a man's life is at stake. Any doubt, regardless how small is beyond reasonable. Based on the many murder cases that are being reversed with new DNA evidence not available at the time of the murder, we have to recognize that we run a high risk of putting innocent men to death. Additionally we should not put people to death who have made a complete turn around in their beliefs. One outstanding example is the woman in Texas that was executed recently after she had turned her life completely around. Many would argue that some will fake a turn around to avoid execution. This argument holds no water however if you put yourself in the shoes of the person in question. What if it were you and you had made a complete turn around and no one would believe that it was real.

In my opinion our prisons need to recognize correction as an option and not just punishment. Once correction has occurred it should be rewarded. Otherwise we throw out everything our law is based on. The Bible, which is the major basis for Western Law, recognizes forgiveness for all sins once we change away from the sin.

Finally three legal foundations need to be changed in both Civil and Criminal proceedings. First is the lack of accountability on judges for their decisions. Second is the limitation on presenting evidence during a trial. And third is the routine practice of asking people to give information about themselves that can be damaging legally.

The lack of accountability on judges for their decisions leads to extremely unfair variation in the way laws are applied. It should be possible to get all decisions reviewed to determine whether they are inconsistent with normal judgments of similar trials. At present, an appeal is not possible unless it can be shown that some legal principle was violated. An appeal cannot be made if the only basis is the verdict. The state supreme courts could be used in such matters to determine whether the judgment is consistent with prudent application of the laws. It would not be necessary to prove that some legality had been overlooked or some legal error had been committed. All that would be needed is a request on the part of the defendant to review whether the decision or punishment was out of line with normal application of the particular laws involved.

In all trial proceedings there are limitations on where and when evidence and arguments can be presented. Because of this a really good lawyer can skew the outcome of the trial by not making it possible for the other side to bring out all their argument. For example the plaintiff has a certain time in which he brings out his side of the argument and the defendant has a similar time. If the plaintiff or the defendant has expended his time they can not bring up additional arguments at a later time. Since the basic intent of the trial is to bring out the truth, this should be changed to permit either party to bring out any new evidence or arguments at a later time even if they have expended their time. Similarly the jury should be permitted to ask questions to clarify any question where the lawyers may have explained only one side of the issue. Admittedly the mechanism for asking these questions may be tricky but at the very least the foreman should be permitted to ask the judge for clarification in writing. It is ridiculous to have your freedom and mine left to the whims and varying skills of whomever we may hire as a lawyer. The foremost principle here is to never punish the innocent if at all possible. Anything that would prevent the truth from coming out should be changed. And at present questions that relate to the guilt or innocence of the accused often go unanswered because of the limitations of the trial proceedings.

Finally, according to the Fifth Amendment we cannot be forced to testify against ourselves. Why then are lawyers and others even permitted to ask us to do so? It should be a fact of law that questions, which would ask us to testify against ourselves, are not permissible. Furthermore questions on job applications, applications for insurance, etc. which ask us to testify against ourselves should not be permitted. Rather than ask someone whether they have committed a felony you should do a background check. Rather than ask someone if they have some preexisting medical condition, you should test for it. The way we currently do things is like giving people speeding tickets based on their answer to a question of how fast they were going. Obviously if the law wants to know whether I was speeding they need to check my speed. Why not make all the other situations just as obvious by not permitting such a question in the first place.

Although I detest the moral ethics represented by the sexual misconduct of Clinton while at the White House, I don't feel it was right to ask him to testify against himself. What if we suddenly decided to go out and ask every man on the street if he had committed any sexual infidelity and then insist on him giving all the details of what he did. While this is obviously absurd, many people see no problem in going up to and asking someone in the public eye just such a question. Martha Stewart should not be going to jail. She should only go to jail because the court has proved she did something illegal. We need to change our posture in the legal community to recognize that such questions are totally out of line. Every lawyer should refrain from asking such questions and every judge should immediately squelch attempts to ask questions of this nature. Additionally it should be illegal to put questions of this nature on any and all applications. The only time questions of this nature should be permitted is when 1) confidentiality is assured such as between a patient and a doctor or between a client and a lawyer and 2) the answer can not be used to penalize the person being questioned.

Chapter 5

WHAT ABOUT ABORTIONS

Common sense has not been used in the abortion question. We have two laws that are in direct conflict and everyone somehow keeps turning their head and ignoring this fact. The first law is that murder is illegal and can not be tolerated. The second law is that it is OK to kill babies in the womb by calling it an abortion instead of murder. Let's apply common sense for a minute.

A few years ago a mother in South Carolina drowned her two young boys. The whole nation was appalled. Did anyone feel that the mother had the freedom to choose whether these children should live? After all they were causing her problems she was unable to handle. Then there was a mother who drowned her five children one at the time. Again we were horrified at a mother murdering her children. How in heavens name are these situations any different than killing a baby in the womb to avoid unwanted problems. Why do we consider one the right of choice while the other is considered murder?

If you were the grandfather to be and you found a doctor killing your grandchild to be, why would you be held accountable for protecting the child with any force necessary. If you were a neighbor and witnessed someone killing your neighbor's kids, would the fact that the neighbor's wife said it was OK release you from the responsibility of protecting the kids?

How are we any better than the Nazi's who stood by letting the Jews be slaughtered simply because the "LAW" permitted it. Common sense, the constitution, all moral bases for the founding of our system of government say there is a law that is higher than man's laws. I am firmly convinced that we will be held accountable for the slaughter caused by our abortion laws.

A simple application of Common Sense brings one to the immediate conclusion that abortion is wrong. All that needs to happen to make this a fact of law is to define the start of life as the time of conception and not the time of birth. Then existing laws take care of the rest of the question. If the unborn child is alive from the time of conception, deliberately taking it's life becomes murder and is punishable by existing law. If the unborn child is not alive how do you explain it's beating heart, it's reaction to pain, it's ability to hear, etc. etc.? Even if you want to define the start of life differently, I am bound by laws higher than man's to protect the unborn. Your error in definition does not release me from my responsibilities. I abhor the behavior of anyone who would take the life of an unborn child and feel any measure to stop such behavior is warranted.

For the crazies who claim the mother has the right to not have the child, let them have their way by keeping the child away from the mother after it is born. If she doesn't want to raise the child, that's fine with me. But don't kill the poor child to accommodate her. The only life she has a choice over is her own. I can understand better her committing suicide to avoid the childbirth than that she kill the baby. Besides if she wants to have a doctor assist with her suicide it could be done in a way to permit the child to live after her death. Those who react in horror to such thoughts are experiencing the same reaction I have to the thought of having an abortion. Only a crazy person would feel that either is proper. Certainly common sense is not exhibited in either case.

Chapter 6

SHOULD COMMUNICATION AIRWAYS BE
TOTALLY FREE

Currently there is a great debate in the country over whether there should be limitations of what someone can say over our communication airways. The first amendment is frequently cited as a reason to lift restrictions. Many argue that censure is bad pointing out that the political party in power could limit criticism against them, etc. Certainly we cherish freedom of speech and history has shown this freedom keeps us strong and free of tyranny. But what about little Johnny sitting down to filth on TV or over the radio. For that matter what about anyone finding themselves overwhelmed with the distasteful programming that is all over the TV.

Looking for parallels, what about the past more conservative eras in this country. It used to be an accepted fact that you not spew profanities over the airwaves. As anyone who has ever been a licensed radio operator can tell you, your license could be lifted for improper words when transmitting. None of these restrictions limited anyone in being able to communicate freely their political or religious views. The only thing these restrictions limited was your choice of words in communicating your ideas.

Part of the problem is certain groups in our society feel like they are being unfairly discriminated against. Homosexuals for example think they should be permitted to practice their sexual habits openly either in public or over the air- ways. People who are very vulgar in their speaking habits don't appreciate having their liberties restricted. Parallels would be speeders not appreciating speed limits and bank robbers and thieves not appreciating laws against stealing. A good way to look at the overall problem is that we need moral codes to prevent moral anarchy just like we need legal codes to prevent legal anarchy. Without some kind of guidelines chaos ensues making it impossible for people of differing views to coexist harmoniously. In this country it makes sense to follow the moral code set down by Judeo-Christian beliefs. A moral code does not carry the same consequences as legal codes. A moral code simply discourages practices outside the code from being practiced openly. It makes it necessary for the participants to avoid unacceptable practices in public where they would be offensive to others. As an example fornication is against our accepted moral codes. But as long as the participants are discreet it has no legal consequences. In the same manner homosexuality which goes against the moral code of the general public is tolerated as long as it isn't done openly where it would be offensive to others.

Looking at the potential gains of permitting vulgarities over the air I fail to see any reason for lifting these restrictions. How do vulgar acts being permitted freely over our communication airways make us stronger. As an example I don't see how use of the F word freely makes communication any freer. It makes it more vulgar, not freer. And say someone wants to strip on stage. How does our not permitting this on the open airways limit free speech. It only makes sure we have speech and actions that are considered to be in good taste. Would we permit someone to urinate in public or perform open sex acts. Then why permit acting that portrays either over our communication airways.

One problem with open communication with no restrictions lies with human nature. All of us, especially during the experimental teenage years, tend to be excited by what's not been permitted before. The lure of forbidden fruit is a real problem for all of mankind. Whatever is not permitted is what we strive to taste. Hence when you open the airways to anything anyone wants to roll out it never stops expanding. For example look at the open discussion and exhibition of homosexuality on all our airways. This would never have been permitted 10 years ago. And what about the sexuality being displayed openly everywhere on TV. Compare what you see today with Elvis' early TV appearances. The change in vulgarity is exponential with everyone trying to go to the next "taste". The reason it continues to get worse is no one is drawing a line and saying it stops here. Until reason is allowed to govern what is permitted over the airways it will continue to get worse. We will see open sex, unlimited vulgarity, and nudity everywhere unless a line is drawn quickly.

Again, looking for parallels in order to come up with a common sense answer, why not look at the societal rules we place on public places. Basically we should not permit over the public airways anything that would not be permitted in a public gathering of reasonable people. If someone wants to be more vulgar than this, let them be restricted to non public places for these acts. Anything that violates these rules should only be permitted in purchased packages. This would permit control over who can make these purchases. Your kids might be able to get these items illegally but at least they wouldn't be exposed to them everywhere they turn the way they are now. This would mean MTV should only be permitted the type of show they could offer at a public gathering. And the same is true of discussions of homosexuality, sexual intercourse, and the type of language being used in any broadcast.

Instead of fining the entertainers for illicit acts, why not pull the license of any station that violates the accepted standards. And the standards should be spelled out in detail. This would mean no transmission of offensive material over the public airways. This is no different than restricting behavior of anyone in public. So far as offensive material, it should be available only through separate purchase that is restricted as to who can make the purchase and it should be distributed only by some method other than the public airways. The long and the short of this is anything going over public airways would be treated as if it were open and in public. Anything that would not be acceptable in public is not acceptable on public airways.

Another parallel for thinking about this is to treat the ability to pick up airborne communications in the same way as our ability to hear or see anything that happens in public. While these rules would make it more difficult for the distributors of offensive material, I don't see how this consideration should trump the very moral fiber of this nation. All the current methods for distributing movies would be available. The profits being made by the distributors of offensive materials would be about the same as now. They just wouldn't be getting all those kids hooked for the future that they hit now from unrestricted distribution.

Chapter 7

DO MEN OF FAITH MAKE BETTER PRESIDENTS

When we vote for a president we try to decide who will do the best job of perpetuating what we feel are the good things in this nation. Certainly we look at such things as how learned he is. And we look at how effective he will be in perpetuating our way of life. Hopefully we vote for the man who demonstrates the greatest wisdom rather than someone who will get us some favor. But should his faith come in to the picture. Many argue that separation of church and state says not to. Others say his faith has nothing to do with how good a politician he may be. What does common sense say?

First off let's define what we mean by the statement Man of Faith. Many people treat this as what church he goes to, which theological truths he ascribes to, whether he never strays into sin, etc., etc. That is not what I mean when I say man of faith. A man of faith is someone who uses his Judeo-Christian beliefs as his basis for thought and action. He may step outside these teachings sometimes but he recognizes this as sin and something he should not do. When he is looking at how to run the country he leans heavily on his faith rather than whether he will have monetary or political gain from his actions. He also has decided that his life is not the all-important thing. His life values are not what he has gained personally but what he has accomplished for his fellow man and how it agrees with his Judeo-Christian teachings. And he has accepted the fact that he is not big enough on his own to solve all of life's problems. It is impossible to do one's vocation without your faith coming to play. It is not a few things you believe but rather the sum total of what you are. Additionally when we say man of faith we know what a man is made of. When we deny that a man is a man of faith we are admitting we don't know what he is made of.

The men who formed the US were mostly men of faith. Did this play a role in making this country what it is today? The evidence is overwhelming that it did. The Judeo-Christian faith has deep-rooted beliefs that have stood the test of centuries. Following the teachings of this faith leads to the unique structure of our US society. Take for example the teachings of some religions that keep men in layered sects as in India and you do not get the same results. The same holds true for communism. The lack of faith of the Soviet society caused them to fail. They had no way to achieve what we have because of their basic beliefs. You may argue that a man brought up in America would know the basics regardless of his faith. But I would argue that you are taking a chance by the very fact that there are obviously some aspects of our societal base that he does not understand. If he is an atheist he does not realize that man's knowledge is not all there is. When a man who lacks faith runs the gamut of what he knows he will not have the deeper basis that a man of faith would have.

We can also look at other countries and political systems for parallel reasoning. Would it make sense for a man of the Judeo-Christian faith to be elected to run an atheistic communistic country like Soviet Russia used to be or China is today. Such a person would almost certainly bring about drastic changes to these systems. In other words if you want to perpetuate a system of government you should elect officials and leaders who have beliefs similar to those who founded the government. Expanding this line of thought to the US you would conclude that we should elect officials and leaders who have beliefs similar to those of the founding fathers of this country.

Another factor is what you know about the man. At least with a man of faith you know his basic beliefs. The important ones that he uses to judge the validity of all those things he's been taught. A man who does not accept the Judeo-Christian precepts is indefinable to a society based on Judeo-Christian principles. Unless you know who his teachers were and how he judged the validity of what he was taught you have no basis for understanding his deepest beliefs. These are the ones that people call on when their own knowledge is no longer adequate. When the situation is larger than the man, and many are, how do you know what he will draw on for strength.

To those of other beliefs these beliefs will appear prejudiced. And some would argue that I should apologize for hurting their feelings or excluding them. I'm sorry but the facts as I see them are that Judeo-Christian beliefs are what made this country what it is today. Those who have a problem with this should ask this question; what role did their beliefs have in making this country great. If their beliefs had nothing to do with it or are of questionable value for us being what we are, they should realize they need to learn from us. If they want to have the benefits of what we've built they should be careful of what they change. It is possible the changes they desire would destroy the very things they like about this country. A man of faith is less likely to make changes counter to his faith.

Chapter 8
DRUG LAWS

I'm convinced the main reason we continue to have laws against drugs is that so many people make so much money from their illegal distribution. The people in the illegal drug business don't want drugs legalized. Their business would be gone overnight. Common Sense dictates that we make drug use legal above a certain age the same way we did alcohol and get rid of the massive criminal organizations that owe their existence to drugs being illegal. Although drug use is a problem, the criminal society caused by making drugs illegal is a much bigger and deadlier problem. Surely we learned from prohibition that you can't legislate morality. Morality can be taught but as we've learned from so many similar situations in the past it cannot be accomplished by force. It seems so good to say that we will stop drinking or drug use through laws but once you look at the end result any thinking person should be able to realize that enough is enough.

Have you ever been to "Crack" City in your town. The squalor and filth and animal type existence is enough to turn anyone's stomach. How can we look on such hideous situations and not realize we need to do something to improve the situation. One of the main reasons such areas exist is that people have to get out of sight of law abiding people to use drugs.

Have you read in the newspapers how many gangland shootings occur daily because of fights between the smugglers and the law or between themselves? Do you not realize that your children through the simple desire to experiment with an enticing sounding substance may actually be risking their lives by who they have to associate with to get the drugs? Have you not lay awake nights with thoughts of what horrible things your kids might someday do for drugs? How is the attempt to punish smugglers through laws worth all this? If the laws were gone these things would no longer happen. For example, you automatically expect drug salesman to carry guns and be at constant battle with the law and other underworld characters. Would this continue if the drug salesman was doing something legal? Would not legalizing drugs erase this scene from every day life?

I don't think any of us want to punish the poor slob who is hooked on drugs. Don't we all want the punishment to be for the people who bring all this about. These guys disappear when drugs are legalized. Therefore there is no one left to punish with all the drug laws when drugs are legalized. Common sense tells us our laws are not accomplishing the thing we wish. It also tells us we are perpetuating the very thing we are trying to eliminate.

I seriously question whether anyone not now using drugs would suddenly rush to use them just because they are legal. If you use drugs now you would continue to but with better quality and without risking your physical and monetary well being. If you don't use drugs now you would still want to avoid them and everyone associated with them as you do now. The main thing that would change is the criminal element behind the drugs would no longer have a reason to exist and you and your children (especially the children) would be safe at last from their violence. Should drug use become a problem after legalizing drugs, laws controlling consumption and actions of the drug user could be initiated to bring about an element of control.

I agree with any of you who say that use of drugs is wrong. I personally have never used illegal drugs and I don't intend to start if they are legalized. I disagree however when you say we need to have laws against their use. The reason is the horrible waste of human life caused by having to work or exist outside the law. Not only are many people killed each year from people fighting for their life in the process of smuggling drugs but many more die from using improperly processed drugs or the squalor caused by living outside the law to feed the habit. And what about the horrible waste of our youth who stoop to prostitution or stealing to get enough money to feed their habit? Sure we feel strongly about use of drugs but should we be risking human life and dignity to the extent it is now risked in drug trading and use.

Chapter 9

IMMIGRATION LAWS

We have a very confused situation in the US over immigration laws. On the one hand we are trying to stop drug smuggling and terrorists having access to our country. But on the other hand we are looking the other way while hundreds of thousands of Hispanics flood the country.

What if during the "cold war" with Russia we had let their citizens come in at will and set up their own systems within our country. It wouldn't have taken long until we would have been in a civil war where the communists were fighting us from within our own country. The analogy with fundamentalist Islam is obvious. What if the cheering for destroying the World Trade Center had been from your next door neighbors or the neighboring city instead of in the Middle East.

So far as protection against infiltration by our enemies, we should restrict visas, etc. to only those countries who agree with our way of life. We can no longer afford to open our borders to citizens of countries known to have hostility toward this country. They don't need to have the right to send students or any one else here. Because of the diversity of weapons of mass destruction any country we don't have absolute trust in should be treated the same way we treated citizens of Communist Russia during the Cold War. Do we question China's right to keep our citizens from entering their borders?

At present any country that doesn't have free elections and any country that has a significant number of citizens who don't like us doesn't need to have free access to our borders. The right to have visitors here should be a favored nation status that is only given out when we know they don't have reason to give support to terrorists. Any country that we even suspect of supporting terrorists should be immediately cut from favored nation status. Countries that don't have favored nation status would then be looking for ways to accommodate our fight against terrorism to gain that status.

I fear that unless we adopt a hard line policy and do so quickly we will soon see millions of our people suffer a much more horrible attack than what happened on September 11, 2001. For example a nuclear weapon detonated in NYC would make the destruction of the World Trade Centers a minor event by comparison. The effect on our economy and our nation would be more devastating than we can imagine. Literally millions of people would be killed or maimed while other millions would be thrust from their homes in a panic retreat to get a safe distance from the radiological hazards. Simply saying we are being harder on our security measures will do no good. We have got to put real teeth into the restrictions at our borders similar to what was used in cold war times against communist infiltration. We've got to realize that the unthinkable is now a real possibility. The terrorist organizations we are at war with will definitely detonate a nuclear weapon in this country if they can get their hands on one. And they won't care about their own personal safety in doing so. Considering the number of countries who now have these weapons and the reduced accountability for these weapons in the countries that made up the Soviet Union it seems certain they either already have one or soon will.

Many measures can be taken to improve our situation. One would be to eliminate drug smuggling by legalizing drugs. This would enable us to concentrate on national security while at the same time shutting down one of the systems that terrorists now use for access to this country and financial support. Another would be to adopt an absolute no trespass policy wherein anyone found in the country illegally would be assumed to be guilty of wanting to bring harm on this country which would automatically land them in jail until they could prove otherwise. Such a policy will make it much easier to police the borders and handle illegal immigration. Illegal immigrants will think twice before bucking these laws which will greatly decrease the number of illegal immigrants. This in turn will help put a spotlight on the ones who are here to bring us harm.

The key here is to assume guilt until proven innocent when it comes to illegal entry into this country. I'm not saying to throw anyone in jail just because they aren't a citizen. What I am saying is to throw them in jail anytime you find them here illegally. Right now we treat these people with the assumption that they are innocent until proven guilty as if they were citizens of this country. That doesn't work when you are dealing with your enemies. We've got to have a way to stop anyone here to do us harm and put them away long enough to prevent them from carrying out their plans.

Chapter 10

CONSERVATION AND GLOBAL WARMING

We have all heard the "Sky is Falling" claims of the conservationists. The conservation movement has done much damage to our ability to construct reasonable laws concerning conservation and pollution by exaggerating the theories of Global Warming and depletion of fuel reserves. This practice of lying and distorting the facts causes great difficulty when the scientific community tries to argue the various aspects of conservation and global warming. When one side feels free to distort the facts the other side appears to be argumentative and hard to get along with as they try to point out that the facts being presented are not really facts.

To illustrate let me describe how one such hoax was presented in the scientific community. I subscribe to Science News, which is one of the best sources for keeping up with what is happening in Science and Medicine. As an example of the cutting edge information they provide I knew about the benefit of aspirin for the heart 10 years before the medical community accepted it. Similarly Science News carried reports of the research on Ulcers which showed bacteria as the cause at least 10 years before the medical community accepted the findings. Yet this magazine which is a banner for reliable scientific reporting carried a major article on pollution and the dangers of global warming that I knew to be a hoax.

The cover to Science News showed a clear crisp picture of the Shenandoah Valley in Virginia back in the 40's during the winter and compared it with a recent picture taken during the summer that showed poor visibilities. The article explained how although energy demands and therefore pollution are higher in the winter the sky back in the 40's was much clearer and free of pollution. The proof they claimed was there in black and white that pollution had increased greatly over the years in a pristine place such as the Shenandoah Valley.

What they failed to mention is a well-known fact to any airplane pilot. On the east coast of the US the air fills with moisture during the summer months and visibility drops from 50 plus miles during the winter to 3 or 4 miles during the summer. In other words the reported proof was totally misleading. No retraction was ever reported. This hoax stood as a scientific study proving how badly we were polluting the air. For anyone who doesn't know the facts about how visibility changes from winter to summer this serves to badly distort the "known facts" about how pollution has changed over the years.

"As everyone knows global warming will cause havoc in Mother Nature with much stronger hurricanes and horrible tornadoes". At least that is what the environmentalist community would have us believe. Actually just the opposite should be true. With global warming the Northern and Southern Latitudes should become more like the tropics. As the differences in temperatures around the globe decrease the cause for storms will be decreased. Temperature differences are what cause storms to occur in the first place. Note I am not professing that we want global warming, I am simply pointing out one of the many exaggerations the environmentalists have made.

How about "we are running out of oil reserves and will soon be destitute with no where to turn for energy". To analyze this theory let's go back to the 17th century when wood was a major source of our energy. Let's put in place massive plans to conserve wood so

we won't run out. Was that really the problem? Of course not.
Now that we use oil in place of wood all that sounds ridiculous.

We have many sources of energy that we aren't even beginning to
tap at this time. If and when we do run out of oil (the reserves
appear to grow rather than shrink so the timing is much farther
down the road than originally predicted by conservationists) these
will then come into play. As one example wind mills placed on our
farmlands could supply all our energy needs by using the power
from them to generate hydrogen, which could then be our fuel.
Another example is nuclear energy. A nuclear reactor sitting on a
body of water could crank out unlimited amounts of hydrogen from
the water to provide fuel. Numerous countries have already taken
themselves off dependency on foreign oil for power through use of
the atom. Still another is fuel from corn and oil from manufacturing
synthetics. The list of known replacements for oil goes on and on.
And after that there is undoubtedly a similar list of replacements we
don't currently know about just as oil was an unknown replacement
for wood in the 17th century.

You may think I am trying to over simplify global warming. Just the
opposite is true. Name me one scientist who knows what caused

the ice ages. Also let him explain when we can expect the next ice age. Until we know the answer to these questions we have no idea what factor man plays in global temperatures. At the moment we don't even know if global warming is occurring. For all we know we could be heading back into another ice age. Although many currently claim global warming is occurring they are at a loss to explain why the polar ice caps are actually growing thicker instead of thinner. In other words the picture is much more complex than the environmentalists claim. Much more needs to be learned before we can make reliable predictions on causes and effects in global temperatures.

Chapter 11

TREATMENT OF THE MENTALLY ILL

Basically our attitude is out of whack when it comes to mental illness. For example the majority of the public feel a divorce is in order when a spouse becomes mentally ill and starts behaving outside the norm. Despite the marriage vows, we treat mental illness as something different from illnesses requiring love and understanding. If that same person comes down with an incurable disease we know what the right thing to do is immediately. We treat mental disorders like alcoholism or physical abuse as if the sick person has a choice in the way they are behaving. But they don't. Since their behavior is out of line, we all seem to feel it is OK to make them an outcast.

Adding to the problem we have excluded the mentally ill from medical coverage by allowing the medical insurance industry to selectively exclude them. Look at your medical insurance. Most likely it either does not cover anyone in your family for mental illness or the limits are ridiculously low to where you will be in immediate financial trouble if any member of your family becomes mentally ill. And the laws on disability don't help because they come into play only when you can't perform any job. The mentally ill usually can hold down certain menial tasks at least temporarily.

The financial ramifications of little or no insurance and our overall attitude of treating the mentally ill as outcasts set the stage for a horrible scenario. First they are dropped from marriages like hot potatoes as the healthy spouse gets in over their head with trying to handle the mental illness. Not only does the mentally ill spouse give you Hell because of being out of their mind but you also find you have no place to turn for help. The cost of medical help quickly gets out of hand moving you toward bankruptcy with no help from the laws governing disabilities. Then everyone around you is convinced you need to get away from the mentally ill spouse because they are treating you so poorly.

Let's look at what can happen if you become severely mentally ill and your spouse leaves you. Soon you will probably do something desperate and someone will convince the medical community that you have to be confined for your safety or the safety of those around you. You will immediately go bankrupt due to the lack of insurance coverage and the exorbitant cost of full time confinement to a psychiatric ward. Then the government body requiring your interment confiscates all you're physical possessions to pay your medical bills and you suddenly have nothing. Next you are deemed "well" because either the cycle of your illness or the treatment while you are confined will show enough improvement that you can be let out. But where do you go? You no longer have anything, you can't hold down a job and all you're loved ones have long since abandoned you. Ever wonder where the homeless come from. Now you know. Sound preposterous like it couldn't possibly happen in America. It happens every day and we sit idly by letting it continue.

Most likely this scenario is due in large part to the horrible sins of the 1800's and early 1900's when people were confined that weren't really crazy thereby stealing their rights. Now the pendulum has swung the other way and there are no real provisions for handling the mentally ill. As soon as they show any signs of normalcy such as a temporary good reaction to medication they can sign themselves out and go free. This is all well and good from the standpoint of personal rights but what about quality of life.

Common sense dictates we rethink the whole thing of how we treat mental illness. First as discussed in the chapter on medical insurance, we need to stop excluding people from health insurance because they are high risk. Mental health should be included the same as any other illness. Second the laws on disability need to be relaxed to recognize that the mentally ill can not hold down a job. The fact that they might could wait tables or clean a bathroom over the short term should not outweigh the fact that they can not hold down the job for any length of time because of unacceptable behavior.

The movie <u>A BEAUTIFUL MIND</u> shows also that we may need to change the way mental illness is handled from a medical standpoint. If the movie is correct, it would appear that collective treatment such as used by Alcoholics Anonymous needs to be explored. Common sense says this should help in that the first thing needed in any kind of healing process is hope. Right now the mentally ill see themselves as hopelessly lost from society. They need to see that they can overcome the illness by the correct reassurance of loved ones and the example of others who have overcome similar illness.

It would appear also from common sense that the whole field of mental health needs to be rethought. It is ludicrous to have the mentally ill homeless and living in squalor. We need to set up a means for those caught in its trap to either work their way out or be able to survive as a human being until that happens. The money end of mental illness needs to be worked out so that we would be satisfied with the set up if it were our selves caught in the trap. The same goes for treatment of the mentally ill by our institutions. They should not be permitted to wander the streets as outcasts but they should be in an environment of their choosing rather than forced into interment. Initially they should be free to come and go to a place of care where they have food and reasonably comfortable accommodations. At some point their decision to live in sub human conditions could be used to force them to stay even if they don't want to. Reasonable behavior could then lead to being free to come and go again until future behavior requires them to be interred again.

Chapter 12
AIRLINE SECURITY

Applying common sense to airline security starts with looking at how similar situations have been handled in the past. The most comparable one to me is the way we handle money using armored trucks. Basically we've already learned how to protect valuables from people who would steal them. And in the final analysis that's all airline hijacking involves. The hijackers are trying to steal the plane for the destruction it can cause or they are trying to steal the plane and passengers to negotiate a point or they are trying to blow up the plane to make a statement. For the first two cases, armored truck procedures should be valuable.

From armored truck security you definitely conclude that the cockpit doors should be impenetrable to hijackers. This would say we need cockpit doors that not only can't be breached by a hijacker but also these doors should not be opened for any reason in flight. And if there is any chance someone could get through the doors the cockpit crew needs to be armed. A marshal in the passenger section would help prevent someone using threats to passengers to get the crew to open the cockpit door.

The last case, a bomb in someone's shoe, luggage, etc. is a different problem. Armored car procedures won't help here since potentially anyone can carry a bomb on board undetected or checked in their luggage. Here we need better security getting on the plane. While metal scanners, random luggage inspection, etc. help, they are not an absolute answer.

We can look to the banks, Fort Knox, and similar places for guidance. One of the most important tools is limited admittance based on security ID. Asking for a driver's license is a waste of time. Why not develop an ID that can be tracked directly to the individual and let you know his citizenship status such as a social security number with a picture ID. These should then be checked by computer against a national database to verify that the number, name, address, etc. match and pick up any flags in the system for specific individuals. The FBI and others who know who to watch out for could then put flags in the system to stop ID's with a questionable background for further questioning and screening. One very important consideration here would be to insist on the cross-check before anyone can board the plane. If the computers go down, other means should be available to permit screening against a national database.

This same ID could use a numbering system that specifies when too little is known about a person due to time in this country, etc. and require additional screening before admittance on the plane. As an example if someone has not been in this country for at least 10 years the ID should show this in the computer base. And foreigners traveling in this country should have to meet much stricter ID requirements. We should not hesitate to hold them up if further information appears desirable. More complex methods of ID such as thumbprints on file at a specific airline could be used for frequent flyers that would permit them access to the plane with less time in line. As long as we hire minimum wage personnel to carry out the security checks, less emphasis should be placed on the ability of the person doing the screening and more should rest on the technology and procedure in use.

As at Fort Knox, anything brought on the plane should be scanned, x-rayed, etc. sufficiently to find a bomb if one is there. If this can not be accomplished with 100% certainty another possible approach would be redesigning the airplane so that an explosion in the luggage compartment would not destroy or disable the plane. From what has been learned with past experience such a design should be possible. Remember the plane in Hawaii that made it safely to a landing after the top half came off. A rear section on the bottom of the plane that blows open preferentially from any explosion in the luggage compartment should leave the plane airworthy and permit the pilot to get it to a safe landing. If such a design is possible carry on luggage should then be eliminated. The insurance companies who have had to pay for past plane disasters would probably offer significant cost advantages for airlines that make these changes and passengers would probably be willing to pay a higher price to fly on this type of plane. Government financing of such a project should not be required.

Chapter 13

COMMON SENSE APPLIED TO CHURCHES

Ever hear anyone say Christianity is dying? What do they base this on? Most likely it's church attendance. So wouldn't it be more correct to say that church attendance is dying? I feel the reason is quite simple. People love to get involved in things where they feel good about what they are accomplishing. People also pour out their hearts and money for good causes. But both church attendance and money given to churches are down. This tells me that people don't feel they are accomplishing good when they go to church and they don't feel the money being contributed to churches is going to a good cause.

If you look at the agenda for most churches they aren't accomplishing a great amount. They are building buildings to worship in and paying the minister. Any "good toward humanity" comes from government programs or private charities. Frankly I feel that what we are seeing is a backlash against such selfish uses of God's money. What is needed is for the church to become the servant of humanity the way it used to be. When it does, attendance will rise and so will the contributions because people will rise to the occasion of God's work.

There are many other signs of sickness in the church. I don't want to appear negative on churches but I feel it will do good to list and discuss some of the things that common sense says needs to change in our churches.

Ministers in the pulpit spend immense amounts of time dotting the i's and crossing the t's of their denomination's theology. The people in the congregation frankly don't care about such detail. Matter of fact if most ministers stood up in the pulpit and insisted that only those who believe as he does stay, the church would be just about empty. Christ criticized the Pharisees for the same tendencies but we don't seem to have learned much in 2,000 years. Does your church preach any of the following:

- Divorce and remarriage is an unforgivable sin

- Divorcees cannot hold any leadership position in the church

- There are no errors anywhere in the Bible

- Once you are saved you are always saved regardless of how you behave

- You're tithe is what you give to your local church and it must be 10% of what you earn before taxes

- Baptism is required or Baptism is not required for you to be saved

- You are a Christian only if you do something that only your denomination does

- Christians should not be involved in politics

First let me suggest that any minister can only answer the above questions with the qualification "personally I believe". Any other answer such as the Bible says or God says can not be proved by studying the Bible. The reason I don't believe any of these can be stated as absolutes is that the answer depends on the background of the person giving the answer. Baptists will answer one way, Church of Christ another, Holiness denominations still another, and so on. If the answer were obvious they would all say the same thing since all of these denominations are truly seeking to know and teach the Gospel correctly. We need to recognize that we may not have the last word on all teachings of the Bible so that we will be open to the correct answer in case we are wrong.

Personally I believe that anyone who is honestly seeking God's Will has nothing to worry about. If your search is motivated by the desire to know and do His will He will lead you to it. Even if you err on the way He will eventually bring you to understand what He wants you to do. The main thing here is to make sure you are submissive to His guidance and not puffed up in arrogance over your own thinking. God is big enough to correct you without the help of ministers or theologians who feel they know the one and only answer to your question. Naturally along the way you should follow the guidance you feel is correct until a better answer comes along. So from time to time you may actually be on an incorrect course because of a misunderstanding of God's teachings. That's why the 10 commandments and similar teachings in the Bible are comforting. At least for the things they cover you know what is right. You have God's direct teaching to tell you in no uncertain terms. Many other things must either be learned from experience or accepted by faith.

Às an example of my thinking let's take the first statement in the list. Divorce and remarriage is an unforgivable sin. For a full discussion of this subject you may want to read my book "THE LAWS OF MARRIAGE". Personally I believe this is not true. Most people that believe this way are quoting Christ's statement in Matthew where He states that to divorce and remarry is to commit adultery. To get from there to the statement that divorce and remarriage is an unforgivable sin you have to believe adultery is unforgivable. As is demonstrated in the New Testament Christ felt that adultery was something that could be forgiven (e.g. the woman at the well). Therefore I personally believe that to divorce and remarry is not an unforgivable sin.

Or another example, many say emphatically that the Bible has no errors in it. The problem with such a belief is that if you think you have found any error in the Bible you throw your whole religion away. I have actually seen some ministers and theologians denounce Christianity simply because they feel they have found some error in the Bible. Common sense says that the Bible should be like any thing else created by man with God's help. Everything else that man has had anything to do with has errors. For the person that steps back and says you either have to believe every word or you can't believe any of it, I say hogwash. God has never been worried about telling us everything. He always leaves it up to us to reason out and fill in the gaps. For example with Abraham He didn't tell Abraham how His covenant would be carried out only that it would come to be true. The same holds true for David. He did not lay it all out for David. He let David operate on faith. And when in the book of Job man was asking why such things as Job's punishment happen God's answer was that we will never understand some things since we are nothing in comparison to God.

The Bible holds together from beginning to end revealing God and His Son through many thousands of years of man's experiencing God. Seeking a second reference in the Bible that supports your conclusion can check any specific words that may be important to you. Hence I have no problem with whether or not there may be some error in the specific words of the Bible. Besides there is one huge source of error that can not be ruled out ever. That is the fact that I may err in the way I interpret what I read. As still another example, many read the lines in the New Testament about ministers should be men with only one wife to mean that someone who has divorced and remarried should not be a minister. Leave the words alone but interpret the husband of only one wife to mean they cannot have a polygamous marriage and the meaning changes entirely.

And still another example is the last statement, which concerns Christians in Politics. First off from the stand point of common sense all you have to do is go back to how this country came into being to see what the truth is. When this country was founded Christians founded it. To have a government then with no Christians in it we would have had to import people of other faiths or atheists to run the country. This would be about as stupid as saying in Israel that there should be no Jews in politics. Who then would run the country. Arabs? I suspect the people who started this belief were atheists who wanted the Christians to give the control of government over to them. It then caught up in the church by circuitous logic that defies common sense. The only Christians who should want to support such a theology would be those who don't want to see Christianity continue in this country. History teaches us that Christians are run off when the government doesn't understand them.

Summing up then, common sense indicates our churches would be better off if they stopped nit picking about theology and got on with doing God's work. Namely the churches should be spearheading work with all kinds of great causes and the Christians from the churches should be very much involved in making this country a better place to live. The church should recognize that the tithe is something that is used to carry out God's work. It is not simply to build buildings and pay ministers. When you look at where we've evolved to, the taxes that go to support welfare, medical research, etc. are part of the tithe needed for God's work.

The ministry should be less a vocation and more a volunteer effort. I'm not saying don't pay the minister. I am simply saying that becoming a paid minister should not be something you learn in school but rather something that evolves from doing works worthy of pay. For example you don't become the president of a large corporation from going to college. Instead you reach that position by work that demonstrates you have the qualities for that leadership role. At present ministry is thought of as book learning largely because that is how you become a minister. It should rather be people of outstanding Christian service who rise to leadership in the church and lead the church into outstanding Christian works.

The tithe should be separated from discussions about church budgets. The tithe is everything Christians give to do God's work. The building fund and the minister's pay should be recognized as just what they are; a small portion of where the tithe goes. For a minister to assert that what you give to your local church is your tithe and therefore should be a tenth of your pre tax earnings is not biblical. If someone wants to give 10% to the local church that is commendable as long as they don't think that's all they need to do to satisfy God's will. But to require it from guilt associated with not tithing is wrong.

Chapter 14

DEMOCRATS VS REPUBLICANS

I thought it might be beneficial to cover the differences between Democrats and Republicans from the perspective of common sense. First off the basis for each is very different. We are not talking two parties who simply have differing views. Rather we are talking about two parties who have a different reason for existence and a totally different approach to looking at things. The republicans represent everyone that stands for. I'll leave it at that. The Democrats represent everyone else. The Democrats basically have adopted the same philosophy that won Thomas Jefferson his election to president. Jefferson simply represented everyone who wasn't represented by the other party.

When you look at the numbers, what happens in the typical election is the Republicans carry the conservative American voters. The Democrats on the other hand represent all minorities and everyone who would be defined as other than the conservative American voter. Hence the Democrats have to maintain a stance of including all the "others" while the Republicans try to run on what they feel the typical conservative American believes.

If you are a Republican and want to win the election your job is to state well what you do believe in. Unless you state your views strongly the people that stand for strong principles won't feel they belong to what you stand for which is their motivation for voting. In stating strongly what you do believe you exclude many minorities who believe differently such as homosexuals. The last election showed the results well. The states that have the least numbers of minorities went for Bush while the heavily populated cities representing the big melting pots for minorities went for Gore.

If you are a Democrat and want to win an election you have to be careful not to say things that will exclude anyone from your party. In other words the Democrats don't necessarily believe the same as all their minorities. They simply are skillful at not excluding them. For example Clinton who was clearly not a homosexual carried the homosexual community by not saying things that would exclude them. To win as a Democrat you have to be careful to say enough that tells each minority you are for what they want while not excluding any other minority with what you believe.

Since Christian views represent the conservative American view, agreeing with the Christian view would run off minorities. Hence the Democratic Party has become the champion of such views as separation of Church and state, abortions on demand, and homosexual rights. If you are a member of one of these minorities it would seem you would be better off with the Democrats. If you don't believe in abortions or homosexuality and you feel Christian views belong in politics you obviously belong in the Republican Party unless you find yourself in some other minority that you feel is excluded by Republican beliefs.

When Clinton was president I heard many Republicans ask the opposing party "why on earth do you vote for Clinton/". Are you a homosexual, do you want to honor abortionists, etc., etc.. They were missing the whole point. The people who voted for Clinton weren't for all of these things. They simply were excluded by some Republican stand or belief. Blacks for example tend to support the Democratic Party because Republilcans make a strong stand against preferential treatment for minorities. All the Democrats have to do to is not over state any stand to the point they exclude the people excluded by Republican beliefs.

Chapter 15

ISRAEL AND PALESTINE

The whole peace problem for Israel and Palestine boils down to the Arabs don't want Israel to exist in their midst period. The problem is one of bigotry and racial intolerance rather than legal land claims. Israel is in much the same position as the American Indian back in the 17 and 1800's when the white man wanted the Indians out period.

The claims of the Arab nations are ridiculous. First they have more land than the United States while the Israelis have a very small fraction about the size of the state of New Jersey. Yet the Arabs argue that Israel should give up some of its land to the Arabs. Although the amount of land owned by the Israelis is quite small compared to the Arab nations the Arabs insist they can't continue to exist with Israel there. Again both are similar to the battle between the white man and the American Indian in the 17-1800 period of America's development. From the analogy with the American Indians it is very important that Israel maintain a superior military capability. Otherwise they will cease to exist as a sovereign nation.

In the past our fear of harming our relations with the Arab nations has held us back from wholeheartedly supporting Israel. Now, in view of what is happening in the war on terror, the time is ripe for just such a stance. Since the Arab countries group Christians and Jews together anyway, we stand nothing to lose with our relations with the Arabs. Our only problem will be within this country. A strong alliance with Israel with joint efforts against terrorists should help bring about respect from Arab countries as will a strong democracy in Iraq. At some time the Arab community is going to have to accept our religious beliefs and those of the Jews. Lasting peace is not possible otherwise. And that time is probably now.

Chapter 16

STOP HOLLYWOOD AT THEIR OWN GAME

Have you ever gone to a movie and come out feeling like someone just dumped garbage all over you. Do you realize that Hollywood makes deliberate efforts to change our moral system. As an example homosexuality has become the little darling of the theater. In movies like the Mexican and Wonder Boys homosexuality is raised to a standard form of romance. As another example the vulgarity practiced in the movies such as use of the F word goes way beyond any reasonable level. And Sex out of marriage is the standard rather than an exception. Etc., Etc., Etc.. Can we find a common sense method to prevent Hollywood from destroying conservative Christian moral values?

Simply writing laws to prohibit poor morality is not the answer. A prime example of this is when Hollywood takes off on a Bible story. Their rendition of Moses in the Prince of Egypt was ridiculous. The only reason the movie gave for Moses leading the people of Israel out of Egypt was to conquer slavery. Not once did the movie credit Moses with simply following the Will of his God. While slavery was an issue, it was not the primary issue of the Exodus of the Jews from Egypt. The primary issue was a people being called by God to take their place in history and reap the blessings promised their forefathers. Restricting Hollywood with laws would not yield a better movie because they can not perform in areas outside their capabilities. They can not become Christian theologians simply because they are doing a movie on religion. And they can not see how ridiculous extremely vulgar language and behavior are as long as they live in such an environment.

The same is true for political views. How can a conservative Christian voter expect to get good guidance from a liberal atheist with respect to how to vote or how the country should be run. Again Hollywood is limited by it's own ability and can not generate true political wisdom just because their story is about politics or the running of the country.

If every other word you speak is the F word and you are writing a script I guess that can be expected to come out in the script. And if you have no moral limitations on sex then it should be no surprise that all kinds of garbage come out in the script. Ditto for those who are homosexual and see no reason for anyone to see that lifestyle as a problem. And as for violence it is simply a cheap way to thrill the audience that should be expected when the writer's skills are too limited to hold the audience's attention otherwise.

It's not that Hollywood feels their view is correct that bothers me. It is that they feel people with the opposite views are incorrect and need to be changed. For example many in Hollywood want badly for conservative Christian voters to change to their thinking. Hollywood would love it if the majority of US citizens held socialistic, atheistic views instead and some will stop at nothing to get this change to happen. Many of the truths conservative Christians hold dear are trounced daily in the movies with a deliberate attempt to change their way of thinking. And Christians pay them to do it, which makes the whole thing ludicrous.

My personal feelings are if these guys want to have socialism as their government model they can find plenty of countries where their view is held. Why don't they go there and leave us with our dirty little capitalistic country that is blowing the doors off every other form of government out there. We are literally fools to continue to let Hollywood use our money to overturn our system of government. If they accept homosexuality as a normal lifestyle, more power to them but stop trying to get everyone else to do the same. And I could go on and on but I won't.

To make a long story short, there is a common sense way to stop this madness. Just about every product produced in this great country carries a money back guarantee. And it's commonly accepted in many fields that money received for services should be refunded if the services are unacceptable. Why not do the same with the movies. Let the FTC hold the same standards for the movie industry that they insist on most other places. We should march to the ticket counter and ask for a refund anytime a movie is not up to our standards. If we're offended by too much violence, inappropriate sex, homosexuality, attempts to sway our political views, etc. we should be able to get our money back. The movie ticket should say satisfaction guaranteed or your money back. Then if Hollywood wants to continue with their attempts to reeducate us they can pay out of their own pockets instead of using our money. It will be interesting to see how long they continue to feel people with views different from theirs need to be reeducated.

Chapter 17
CHRISTIAN OUTREACH

Many fear Christianity because "they" are always trying to convert the world to their religion. In Islam for example one can be sentenced to death for trying to convert someone from Islam to Christianity. Most non-Christians will tell you immediately that Christians are no different than all the other religions in that their insistence that they are right has led to many wars. John Lennon wrote in his songs about how wonderful the world would be if there were no religion and there were no Heaven or Hell.

Being a Christian myself it is very difficult to see all these criticisms objectively. However common sense can be used to reason whether these criticisms are valid. First off what is Christianity. Let me give it a very simple definition that everyone will agree with immediately. Christian behavior is to behave the same way Jesus Christ would. The slogan WWJD (what would Jesus do) is in reality the best way to determine what a Christian should do.

Using this definition Christianity should not be invasive and it should not cause wars. When the Jewish theologians arrogantly questioned Christ on whether he was following God's law or tried to trick Christ with loaded questions, Christ handled their questions with authority and showed they were in error.   But anytime someone was seeking to know God's will He was gentle and kind in His teaching.   Christ never forced His will or thinking on the people of the world. Basically if you wanted to disagree with Him He did not get upset with you or try to force you to think His way.   He changed people by His example and gentle statements of what is right and what is wrong based on God's teachings in Jewish law.

The Gospels teach in John 3:16 that Christ died for our sins and as a result if you believe in Him you will not perish but rather have eternal life. While this says if you don't believe in Him you may go to Hell, Christ would never have come out in a fire and brimstone fashion saying "you will go to Hell if you don't believe in me". And John 3:17 which comes right behind the statement of salvation says "For God sent NOT His Son into the world to condemn the world; but that the world through him might be saved".

Where many Christians get in trouble with outreach is they try to apply Christianity as a tool for judging others. While Christianity definitely can be used to tell us where we personally may be going astray, it cannot be used to judge whether someone else is in error. I feel that as long as someone is truly seeking God's will they will find it. Like Christ we have to be patient and let them work it out with God the same way we did. As an example most would readily say that Judas was not saved and surely went to Hell. But would you not agree that his final act of suicide after betraying Christ showed that he was truly sorry for what he had done. And this act indicated he believed Christ was the savior. I am not saying one way or the other whether he was saved. I am simply pointing out that his salvation was between him and God.

To understand further how Christ behaved in outreach look at the fact that He could have easily forced His views on all that listened. For example He could have used miracles or angelic intervention to force recognition of who He was. He and His disciples could have openly threatened everyone to either believe in Him or plan on going to Hell. He could have used fire and brimstone speeches or for that matter even called down fire and brimstone. In other words he could have behaved much more strongly than those who try to force the Christian message on people today since He was the prime authority for all such thought. But He didn't.

Applying this thinking to Christian Outreach would say we likewise should not be invasive in our teachings and we should not try to force someone to change to Christianity. Just as Christ was infinitely patient with the people of His time we should do the same today. Words such as "you are going to Hell if you don't believe in Christ" etc. should never come out of the mouths of those seeking to spread the teachings of Christ. Instead the teaching of the Gospel should be stated in a positive way; Christ died for our sins so that whoever believes in Him should not perish but have eternal life.

The main teaching of the bible about our dealings with man is the Golden Rule. Do unto others as you would have them do unto you or love your neighbor as yourself. This teaching must be applied to Christian outreach or you end up fighting with all who are not of the Christian faith. By the way one of the major problems of Islam is it does not have this teaching. Basically every other major religion other than Islam teaches the golden rule. Instead Islam teaches you to love your fellow Moslem but not your neighbor. This is one of the primary reasons Islam expels all other religions from its lands since the infidel's views or rights do not matter. This of course results in war-like thinking for its followers. If one assumes that any major religion should lead to peace and understanding for all mankind, Islam would fail to qualify.

Chapter 18

AFFECTS OF THE INTERNET ON POLITICS

The day when politicians are unable to determine what their constituents want is behind us. Once the political climate permits, the computer and the internet will permit the political community to poll their constituents at will. And at the same time each of us will be able to communicate our feelings easily. What has to happen first is the political community will need to let go of the current lobby system, which is full of perks and money. And A few strong congressmen will need to pioneer the improvement in communication possible here. The lobbies will try to avoid the improved communication possible on the internet since this type of communication is more difficult to manipulate to give desired results. But the congressmen who champion this cause will gain much in the public eye and make a real name for themselves.

Now that just about everyone owns a computer, polling of constituents can be done fairly easily. Each congressman can post questions to issues they want input on using their web site. These web sites can then collect responses from anyone who wishes to give their views. Social security numbers can be used to verify that the response is truly from the person indicated and protect against multiple responses.

Such a system will not be without problems. People wanting rule by majority vote of the public instead of informed votes by congressman will be tempted to go further and require voting only by polling the constituents. Congressman will then have the problem of explaining why they went against the views of the majority if they feel the need to do so. The news media and others who don't recognize the need for mature judgment that over rides the majority will become a challenge. But on the plus side it can become a means for everyone to get much more involved in the affairs of government. And also on the plus side the increased communication will make it possible to demand much more accountability from your congressman.

From the perspective of the internet, the day of the town meeting has returned. Although it won't be possible for everyone to give input in their own words, properly structured web site polls can be used to bring out everyone's views. In the past the avalanche of responses by voters often reflected only how hard the lobbies had worked to get constituents to send in mail or petitions or similar communications to their congressman. Such an avalanche of responses could be very misleading. Now with the internet the responses should better reflect the true view of a congressman's constituents.

Once our congressmen start using the internet more, their web site can be used not only to poll their constituents but also to keep their constituents informed of what they are doing. For example Web sites can devote as many pages as necessary to explain the congressman's views on major or controversial issues. They can also be used to show how he has voted on past issues, how he plans to vote on future issues, what he feels is important to his constituency, etc. Voters can then be better informed by going to the congressman's web site to get it straight from the horse's mouth so to speak. Congressmen who don't want to keep their constituents informed will suffer at the polls once the internet becomes a strong political tool.

Chapter 19

PREVENTING ABUSIVE BEHAVIOR
IN CHILD CARE CENTERS

For years we've all read about and been horrified by sexual abuse that occurs in many child-care centers. And we all wonder if our children are being treated well by the child care providers we leave our children with.

The problem stated another way is how do you prevent someone from doing things behind your back that you would not permit if you knew about it. Convenience stores have a parallel problem. Shoplifters stealing merchandise when you aren't looking or someone robbing the store. Convenience stores solved this problem years ago. They simply use video cameras throughout the store.

Why not require video camera coverage of all activities concerning children in day care centers. Anyone deliberately taking a child outside the range of video coverage could be subject to immediate dismissal. Sound too strict? We do this for convenience stores; why not for our kids? If it sounds too expensive think of the expense of one child abused. The well being of a child is certainly worth a lot more than the cost of goods that are stolen from a convenience store. If it sounds too restricting to personal freedoms, it's no different than allowing the parent to stay and watch their child while he is at the child-care facility. So why don't we wake up and solve this problem once and for all.

It should be obvious why Uncle Sam has not been able to solve this problem. First He has two opposing views; the owners of the day care centers will feel the solution is too expensive and too demanding on their business while the mom and dad with kids at the day care want added protection against abuse. Why on earth do we need to wait for Uncle Sam? All we need to do is demand this as a minimum from our day care providers. The wise day care owners will use the installation of video equipment as a selling point for their business. It will then become popular to protect the children and through popularity it may become law.

An added advantage of videos would be to permit parents to check whether the care providers are doing their job well for whatever reason. For example if little Johnny starts acting strange there would be a way to check whether the child- care center is the source of the problem.

The use of a common sense device like video cameras can be beneficial many other places.   They can help anywhere they would prevent people from doing things behind your back you would not approve of.   The list is much too large to cover all examples but a few are discussed below.

In the school system it would accomplish protection for teachers and students who are being abused by bullies in the classroom. One reason students act unruly is they are in a system where no one cares. They feel like they can get away with "murder" because no adult who knows them will see. I know because in growing up in a large metropolitan area we had no fear of doing bad things because no adult who knew us would see.   When I moved to a small town, you just didn't do things like that any more because word would get back home. Videos in schools would go a long way towards correcting this problem.

Police vehicles should be equipped with video equipment also. It can help prevent people (including the police) from doing things they wouldn't do if they knew someone would see them. And it could be valuable in other situations also. Have you ever been accused by the law of doing something you didn't do? If you have you will wholeheartedly agree with the next suggestion. Since everyone including a policeman can make a mistake, your word should be treated as equal to his in a court of law. Several times I have been in court where a policeman disputed my word and the judge or jury took the word of the policeman over mine. In each case I had told the truth and the officer had been mistaken over what he had seen. Why not require a second witness or video evidence to decide these cases. This should drastically reduce the number of innocent people mistakenly found guilty.

There are other abuse situations where common sense would eliminate the problem. Take sexual harassment in the office place for example. Videos are not a very good tool to prevent sexual harassment. Since these situations occur anywhere and anytime, preventing them by video would require that we be under a video camera all the time. This would be too much like BIG BROTHER IS WATCHING. However there is a much better way to handle sexual harassment than HIS word against HER word. At present employers have to decide scenarios of whether she is telling the truth and he should be fired, etc. etc.. This is totally unnecessary.

When accusations of this nature start occurring, why not use a little common sense and simply arm the victim with a small tape player that all parties know about. This will either stop the harassment or prove the guilt or innocence of the person being accused. In the case of a woman by herself with someone abusive, she could carry a small tape player in her pocketbook that would prove her side of the story whenever she wanted to bring a stop to the abusive behavior.

Again, a large part of the reason we aren't solving these problems is we are so used to Uncle Sam doing our thinking. These are situations where Uncle Sam can not do as good a job as we can. None of these are difficult to reason out. All are simply in need of a little common sense.

Chapter 20

SUCCESS AND EDUCATION

We have all heard the saying "to get ahead you need to get a good education, get a good job, and work hard". This sounds fine but most people who've gone this route will readily tell you it doesn't work. For example many of the wealthiest people in the United States have only a marginal education. Matter of fact there is another saying that you hear at college that says " the A students will end up teaching the B students how to work for the C students". My observation would be that the latter statement is much truer than the first. A students get hired by the colleges and universities to be teachers. The B students end up getting jobs in industry. The C students realizing they are on the bottom of the ladder start a business of their own in self-defense. And in this scenario the C student will end up more successful than the A and B students.

Another observation on success in America is that people coming to America from a foreign country often have the biggest most successful businesses. I submit that this is true because we blindly grope along from school to job thinking we will get ahead that way while people from other countries recognize the freedoms available here and capitalize on them by going into business for themselves.

The schools do not teach what is required to get ahead. One of the major secrets is to leverage your time or money using other people's time or money. Going into business for yourself you immediately set yourself up to leverage your time through the people you hire. At the same time you may find you are able to leverage your money by getting loans or by selling stock such that you are using other people's money. Getting a job you find you are paid for your time only. You are literally trading your time for dollars. Without a doubt the wealthiest people in this country are the ones who have built successful businesses rather than people who simply have a job working for someone else.

Another major secret to success is your attitude and your self-image. Name me one school system in America that teaches this. Dale Carnegie with his book "HOW TO WIN FRIENDS AND INFLUENCE PEOPLE" and David Schwartz with his book "THE MAGIC OF THINKING BIG" cover these subjects extremely well. Yet neither book (nor a reasonable substitute for that matter) appears in the list of books used in our school system.

At present the logic of the school system is to teach students the mechanical skills needed to perform a job. Why in the country with the greatest opportunity in the world are we so narrow-minded?

We should be teaching students what it takes to have a business of their own and what the advantages of doing so are. We should also be teaching the importance of attitude, self-image, and people skills. It is unforgivable to graduate students from High School and College who don't have a clue about what it takes to succeed. This wouldn't be so bad in a country where you don't have the freedoms to go after anything you want in life. But it is a crime in this country.

Additionally we have entered a sad era in our school system where the teachers are being led to believe that the problem with our education system lies almost entirely with the students. The medical community for example has done our children a tremendous disservice by inventing the label hyperactive. Children that were recognized as a challenge for teachers a few decades ago are now being given drugs by their pediatrician to make them easier for the teacher to handle. Instead of drugging the kids we should be training the teachers how to handle these kids. The information I have suggests that hyperactivity is not a problem for these kids later in life. Matter of fact most of these kids are very well liked when they go out into the working world and frequently exhibit personality traits that help them get ahead of non hyperactive kids in their careers.

Similar problems have come about from labeling kids as uneducable, mentally slow, etc. Several schools have sprung up in the center of challenged areas such as downtown Chicago and downtown New York that prove the problem with such labels is with the teachers and not the students. The solutions found go back to well-known principles, which are apparently not being taught well in colleges who are preparing our teachers to teach. Sound principles of discipline fairly applied in a positive uplifting manner usually correct the discipline problems. Teaching a good self-image and positive possibility thinking usually correct the learning problems.

It is my feeling that children are the same today as they were in earlier years when we didn't have these problems. The problem is with the way we are teaching our teachers and the changes we have made in the school system. We now do things routinely in our schools that families would never have permitted at home in the past. Any time you have a family with no moral foundation to what they teach their children you have big problems. The schools by no longer extending basic family morals to school life have invited the same problems. Encouraging kids to do things at school that their family would not permit such as handing out condoms, eliminating any mention of Christianity, encouraging abortions, etc. hurt rather than help the kids.

As you'll see in more detail in the next chapter I feel it's time we stop apologizing for who we are and what we believe in this country. By not using the guidelines of the religion that helped shape the moral fiber of this great country we don't help anyone. We instead eliminate any semblance of reason to our moral code and throw it out the window. It is about the same as saying that we are afraid of offending criminals by having laws so therefore we will have no more laws in our schools. We all recognize this would cause anarchy. We need to recognize the same thing happens at the moral level generating the equivalent of anarchy when you have no basis for your morals.

So far as weak teaching is concerned, we need to learn from the few examples of excellence in teaching now going on. Once understood, the practices that are making these systems work need to be used throughout the country. Rather than spend billions to get the number of students down so the teacher is closer to each individual student, we need to get the practices of the teacher improved so they are more effective on any scale. After all it doesn't help little Johnny one bit to get him down from 1 in 40 to 1 in 20 if his teacher is negative in her impact on him. If she is telling him how he can't do something for example he is better off in the larger class.

Chapter 21

RELIGION, LANGUAGE, AND OTHER THINGS
TO BE PROUD OF

If you go to Jerusalem do you expect the Jews to avoid mention of Judaism in their schools, and government offices? How about in India, Saudi Arabia, etc., etc.. Yet here in this country we avoid mention of the religion that helped shape this country. Christianity was unquestionably the basis for most of the laws and moral structure of this country. Although we have become the greatest country in the world we act ashamed of one of the major reasons we have achieved such greatness. We have people even going so far as to say that Christians should not participate in our government.

I have heard the argument repeatedly that we are required by the constitution to keep Church and State separate. Actually the constitution says nothing about people practicing Christianity. All it speaks of is the State making people practice one religion such as Christianity over another. For those who say that Christians should not even participate in politics, this is as preposterous as the Jews refusing to have any one of the Jewish Faith in their government.

106

For America at the time of it's founding and for Israel now, the only way you could satisfy such a ridiculous rule would be to import people from other countries to run the country.

Instead of apologizing to everyone for who we are, we would be much better off to let them know who we are so they can understand us. It's time we be proud of our heritage and let others see that pride. If our majority religion were Hindu I would expect to see Hindu references throughout our culture. By not letting the major religion show, we are hiding who we are and dropping the primary basis for our moral structure. As I said earlier, this would be about the same as not having any laws for fear they might offend law-breakers. Anarchy results either way by people not having guidelines to go by.

When Jimmy Carter took office he apologized for everything about America's greatness. He got people to think in terms of not being the greatest power on earth, not having the richest nation, needing to conserve because we were running out of fuel supplies, etc. We had long lines at the gas pumps, rationing of gas, government guidelines that demanded we turn down our thermostats in the winter, less expensive cars being driven by our leaders, etc.. This country started a nose-dive, our economy went into runaway inflation, we suffered major shortages in fuel supplies, and everyone said it would never be the same again. Everyone basically said no one could ever correct all the problems we had. We just as well get used to having them.

When Ronald Reagan came into office he took just the opposite stance and suddenly all the problems that had been impossible to solve were miraculously solved. Conservation disappeared as more aggressive measures were used to generate ample reserves of fuel, the long lines at gas stations disappeared, thermostats returned to reasonable settings, etc. etc. Double-digit inflation disappeared and so did the Berlin Wall. And this country was suddenly recognized as the greatest power on earth.

What I see from this is the importance of us being proud of who we are and what we stand for. I don't mean arrogant in the sense of the ugly American. Just proud in the sense of a great self-image. Anytime someone has a poor self-image he performs below par. And that holds doubly true for a nation because a nation like a sports team is constantly in competition with other nations around the world. Basically my view is that anyone who dislikes knowing what makes this great country tick, including religion, can go anywhere else in the world they choose to get happy.

In the same vein, when someone moves to Germany they should not expect everyone there to learn their language. In the case of English, most people recognize it is a good thing to learn since America is the leader of the free world. But otherwise you would not expect the people of the other country to know or learn your language. And if you constantly spoke in a language that no one there understood you could expect to be on the outside looking in. I feel the same is true for foreigners moving to this country. We are expressing a lack of good posture when we start putting everything in the second language. And we are paralyzing the new citizens from a foreign country when we do this because they would be much better off knowing English.

Finally on this subject, September 11 brought back the pride I'm speaking of. We no longer apologize for the prayer to open a meeting or a pledge to the flag. There for a while a lot of us were growing very concerned from the lack of pride In America and the way we were apologizing to everyone about who we were. When Roseanne disgraced this country with the vulgar way she sang the national anthem she represented what this country was coming to. Thank God we have risen from that muck and made what appears to be a full recovery. We now need to remember how important it is to know who we are and what we stand for and be proud of both.

Chapter 22
FAMILY

The family is without question the basic unit for our society. The stronger the family is the stronger the nation will be. Right now the family is under attack as never before. We were horrified at the definition of family offered by communist Russia in its heyday of threatening to conquer us. The communist definition of family was that the state owned the family and the state would be the protector of the individuals of the family. Compare this with where we are today in this country and you will see that we have come dangerously close to the communist definition.

Divorce is rampant causing destruction of the basic family unit. The schools are insisting that our children have rights outside the family and therefore the state should be their protector. As examples of this:

· Christianity is forbidden in the schools leaving the children with no   moral guidance.

· Condoms are handed out freely without the permission of the parents.

· Abortions are carried out without letting the family know.

• Children are being drugged for ADD to make it easier for the teacher to control them.

• DSS stands as a constant threat to parents and grand parents should anyone accuse them of unnecessary force when disciplining their children.

• Gays are threatening the very fabric of the family by their ludicrous insistence on enforced acceptance of their warped sense of what sex is. Their very existence defies the definition of family since they can't generate off spring.

We even have courts permitting children to get a divorce from their parents.

So far as divorce is concerned, we need to get back to the real definition of family. Marriage is simply an artificial means of becoming a member of a family. Once the marriage has happened the partners need to recognize their role is irreversible. We all recognize that our son or daughter is forever our son or daughter regardless of how they behave or what they become. The same should be true for your wife or husband. Lets say your son becomes sick, disabled, mentally ill, bad mannered, ill tempered, an outlaw, or in any other manner someone who is not as healthy, capable, or desirable as you would like him to be. Does he stop being your son? Do you suddenly claim someone else as your son? Of course not. How is this any different if the person in question is your spouse?

The reason we have so many divorces is two-fold. First we have elevated happiness to a right. And second we constantly make the mistake of going to a lawyer when things aren't good which pushes the divorce from impossible to possible status. Happiness doesn't come from doing only the enjoyable things in life. True happiness comes when we live up to our responsibilities and do the right thing. Using a lawyer when you are in a marriage squabble is very dangerous. The role of a lawyer is to expound on your rights and what you want. Since what you want and what your disgruntled mate want are always going to be at odds in a squabble, using a lawyer leads to the only conclusion possible. That is to separate from your mate so you no longer have to fight for your rights and what you want.

Unfortunately we are not going to be able to legislate proper behavior in a marriage regarding divorce. Instead we need to increase public awareness of the importance of family and how to have a successful marriage.

Since this country was founded on Christian principles and since our laws and moral standards come from these principles, there is nothing wrong with permitting Christianity on school grounds. To do otherwise leaves anyone growing up in our society totally ignorant in a very important area. All kids graduating from our school system need to know what makes us tick. Otherwise they will be stupid and unskilled in areas that will cost them dearly throughout life. Look at the schools that tried to teach Islam as a result of 9-11. It's millions of times more important that we understand our own community than it is to understand some foreign community. How would it have been prior to World War Two if we had permitted the teaching of Axis power beliefs but not our own in the school systems? Just think, we could have had the wonderful result of not having to fight that war. We could have simply understood the enemy over ourselves and surrendered when the war broke out.

The laws putting the state above the family need to be rescinded. Until a child reaches the age of 16 or 18 they should be the sole responsibility of the family. Anything a school may want to do for our children should require parental approval first. And any parent who cannot get satisfaction from the school on this should be permitted to remove their child from that school and place them anywhere they desire whether it be another public school, home schooling, private school, etc.

DSS should never be permitted to put the state over the family in the care of a child. If the parents are doing something harmful and illegal to a child such as child pornography, sexual abuse, or physical abuse, the parent can be charged with the crime and corrected accordingly but the state should not be given the role of taking the child away from the parent. No matter what the parent may be doing they continue to be a member of the family and no matter how great the state may be they can not become a member of the family. Rather than have the state assume this role, members of the children's family should be sought first to care for the child when their parents can't. If there are no family members who can provide care or in cases of extreme harm to the child from their parents, emergency provisions should be made to provide for the child's welfare. But still the state should not be given custody of the child. Instead family oriented establishments such as churches, foster homes, and similar organizations should have temporary protective custody until more permanent arrangements can be made. The more permanent arrangements should again come from family oriented establishments rather than a state organization.

With regard to the gay community we need to stop elevating their selfish goals into legal requirements. If they want to live together that's fine but not if you have to destroy the definition of family and marriage by changing the laws concerning marriage and family before this can happen. If they want to not be discriminated against they need to recognize that their behavior is unacceptable in public and keep it private. There are no laws that can make the straight community accept homosexual behavior as normal. All you have to look at is how we are designed sexually to accept this as fact. To do otherwise would be like forcing people to accept females as the same sexually as males. It just is not going to happen. Protecting the gays with anti discrimination laws that encourage unacceptable displays of homosexual behavior in public is like making it legal for the straight community to have sex in public.

I see nothing wrong with a stance that recognizes homosexuality as an enemy of the family unit. As such this type of behavior should be treated the same as pornography, sex outside of marriage, adultery, etc. and tolerated only when it is done discreetly and out of public view.

Chapter 23

SOCIAL SECURITY

I don't know what the original rules for setting up our social security system were. What I do know is the way it works now. The money put in each year by those of us looking forward to our future is used to pay the people who have reached their retirement years. Common sense is not necessarily a way to come up with the best way for Social Security to be set up but it certainly can be used to analyze whether the current system or a proposed new system is adequate for the future.

While the baby boomers were coming into the market place their overwhelming numbers made the system work for today's retirees. But now that the numbers are reversed it is about to fail. There is no way for the small numbers coming into the market place to support the large numbers from the baby boom generation who are about to retire.

The only way to guarantee that a given generation will be taken care of fairly is to have it support itself by it's own investments. The problem right now is we haven't invested previous moneys so there is no investment waiting for us when we retire. The problem is going to be playing leapfrog from a system that is about to fail to a new system that will work.

All the arguments being presented are confusing. Some say we are destroying Social Security or robbing retiring America by not giving them what they are due. While it is true that the system is about to fail, it is not true that anyone is being done in by choice. The failure is from lack of planning over the last decade or two.

Others say we need to change to an investment-based system. That this will save our social security system. Unfortunately we still have to make up for the lack of investments for the upcoming baby boom generation that is about to retire.

It is safe to say that the solution will have to incorporate both aspects. First it will have to incorporate a way for the baby boomers to have a retirement income. Second it should shift to an investment-based system where each generation takes care of itself by making proper investments over that generation's lifetime. Those who fear investments such as the stock market for retirement benefits fear the very basis of our financial system.

Either a safe way can be found to bring about substantial growth of pension funds for retirement purposes or our whole monetary system is a hoax.

One thing most people over look in investing for the future is inflation. Since inflation is constantly with us, we have to invest in a growth fund that will at least keep up with inflation. Otherwise the moneys laid back for retirement will be too small to live on. Basically the cost of everything doubles every 10-15 years. When I was 20 years old you could buy a car for $2,000. Forty years later you can't buy a similar car for less than $20,000. The same is true for housing and the cost of living. Hence unless your investments grow the money you set back shrinks in buying power.

One thing common sense tells us is we need some form of national system to insure against large numbers of people having no way to survive when they retire. Many people simply will not save for the future if it is left up to them. And it is not fair for those who do save to have the burden of taking care of those who refuse to. Another thing common sense tells us is we should not take money from industrious people unless we give them a fair return on their investment. To do otherwise is robbing those that would save to benefit those who refuse to and doing it so poorly that neither gets a reasonable benefit from it. In other words the one who would otherwise be responsible and save his money should not be done in by a system that is irresponsible.

The reason no one is offering a hot plan for fixing the social security system is no one knows how to spend the money coming in to support retirees and invest the money for the future at the same time. It simply can not be done. Hence any plan offered must incur the penalty of making up for past errors while at the same time preventing similar errors in the future. Criticism of the current system is a waste of time. It is about to fail. We need to stop the blame game that politicians are engaged in and get on with solving the problem. Although each political party blames the other for the problem, the fact of the matter is everyone is to blame for letting an improper system to continue for decades. What is needed now are proposals that admit to the upcoming failure while offering solutions. And even though the discussions may be unpleasant, our congress needs to get serious about putting a new system in place.

Chapter 24

PHILOSOPHY 101

Our scientists and theologians understand everything about mankind, both past and present, or so you'd think when you get into philosophical arguments about where we come from and where we are going. But do they really know us? My experience would say we know very little about ourselves.

For example was there a great flood as talked about in the Bible and most religions. People will argue about this for days one proving it is all myth and the other proving it really happened. The slant on the argument usually comes from personal bias instilled by our religious beliefs. People who think the bible is a mythical teaching are convinced that a worldwide flood is preposterous. While people who believe the bible look to scientific evidence for an ark and anything else that would support the story.

Let's look at it from a common sense point of view for a moment. We all know that the earth was virtually submerged in ice from a worldwide ice age. We can also reason that the ice on land came from water that was part of the seas. We can further see that large swings in sea level caused by water becoming ice would have left huge expanses of land dry that would later be flooded. Even further we know that the writings of the bible and most religions come from populations that lived around the Mediterranean Sea. It doesn't take a rocket scientist to carry all this one step further and at least accept that the known world at the time of the ice age would have experienced one whale of a flood as the ice melted. So it's really no wonder that the ancients mention a great flood and biblical stories of a flood are not far fetched at all.

The bible talks about God speaking everything into existence. We all know how preposterous this all sounds because things don't just appear out of thin air. Or do they? Science, which is man trying to explain what he finds in nature, says otherwise. Einstein's theory of relativity says that matter (things) comes about whenever energy (thin air) comes to rest. And the reverse is true. Whenever matter disappears it generates huge quantities of energy, which is the basis of atomic energy. Carrying all this to its ultimate meaning, the whole universe balances out to be one great big nothing. If all the matter in the universe comes back together (it is supposedly comprised of equal amounts of matter and antimatter), it will all revert back to energy and there will be no more anything. So to make a long story short, the statement that God spoke everything into existence sounds like a pretty good description of what the universe really is.

Many people are totally wiped out at the thought that anyone would consider the possibility of a virgin giving birth. This proves to the agnostic that the whole Christian thing is ridiculous. Come on guys. Doctors cause virgin births all the time now. Look at artificial insemination, man's work in cloning animals, etc. etc.. If Doctors can do this with ease why is it so far fetched that God can do such things.

We are the most advanced civilization the world has ever known. Or so we are taught in school. If so, why are there so many things that men were able to do 4,000 to 10,000 years ago that we can't begin to explain or duplicate today. The statues of Easter Island, the Sphinx and the pyramids of the Middle East and similar structures in Central and South America, Stone Henge, and many other mysteries of the ancient past. A lot of these at first glance appear to be something we could do today. But close investigation reveals stone cutting that would require the use of diamond blades, precision in astronomy that far exceeds current abilities, and many other anomalies. I have no theory about the meaning of all this.

My only point is that there is a tremendous number of things we just don't understand. And we should not get too puffed up about our ability to explain everything.

Everyone knows the bible does not teach re-incarnation. Or at least that's what I've been told all my life. However this seems to be another "truth" that may not be true. If there is no teaching about re-incarnation in the bible, then what is Christ talking about in the New Testament when He says that Elijah has already come back in the form of John the Baptist. Also from the bible we all know that people who have died and gone to the spirit world can not communicate with the physical world. At least that's another teaching I always heard growing up. If this is true, who were the people with Christ when He was in the garden praying the night before He was crucified? And then there is the instance in the bible where Saul uses a medium to call up the spirit of Samuel. Saul and Samuel actually carry on a conversation after the medium calls up his spirit. Again My only point is that there is a tremendous number of things we just don't understand. And we should not get too puffed up about our ability to explain everything.

"If it's MLM I'm not interested" meaning of course that if an opportunity in question is multi-level marketing it can't be any good. Such clichés show ignorance on the part of the speaker regarding how business works. Virtually every business in America works like an MLM whether it is DuPont or the Catholic Church. All have a head and all have an organization stemming from the head that generates a working business organization. There is a major difference between a MLM and a normal business for someone entering the business. The normal business already has a structure with the owner and management being the only ones who benefit from other people's time. The MLM on the other hand offers new entries a way to start out at the top of their own organization regardless of how long the business has been in existence.

The correct business question when looking at an MLM is not whether it is an MLM but rather what is it's current and projected growth potential. When Sam Walton started Wall Mart it didn't look too promising but his business, which is structured like an MLM as all businesses are, did fine. The same is true for Rich Devos and Jay VanAndel with Amway. Both Wall Mart and Amway made the owners billionaires and both generated a large number of millionaires in the ranks as they grew. Amway is not inferior due to being an MLM. They both have the same structure when you analyze how they grow and both businesses have the same potential for growth.

They both offer the participants wealth at the top but Amway offers entry-level participants a greater opportunity to reach the top since everyone entering Amway comes in as a business owner while everyone entering Wall Mart comes in as an employee. Business owners have the advantage of leveraging their time by benefiting from other people's time as well as their own. Employees on the other hand don't receive this benefit until they work their way up into higher management. As an employee they make money only as a straight exchange of hours for dollars with no way to leverage their time.

Said another way, someone who is ambitious and wants to get ahead will do better in Amway since they will be able to immediately leverage their time by bringing other people into the business. And their growth is limited only by their willingness to continue to find people who want to work with them. Someone who just wants an hourly wage will do better at Wall Mart since they are paid just for being there a certain amount of time each day doing whatever the boss wants. To get ahead in a business like Amway all you have to do is take the time to find people who want to be in business with you and then help them build a business. To get ahead in a business like Wall Mart you have to first please the boss and get him to feel that you are more qualified than the other workers around you so you will get promoted to management. Either business requires you to leverage your time from other people to become wealthy.

Printed in the United States
30327LVS00004B/208-228